Spaghetti on Mondays

Tom Flaminio

Dodici Publishing, LLC

Spaghetti on Mondays

Tom Flaminio

Published by Flaminio, Tom.
Copyright ©2011 Tom Flaminio
Dodici Publishing, LLC

Cover by Stephanie Lake, Globe Printing
Interior Layout by Stacey Willey, Globe Printing
Edited by Georganna Hancock and Bonita Kale

Printing Coordinated by
Globe Printing, Ishpeming, Michigan
www.globeprinting.net

First Printing April 2012

ISBN 978-0-9850299-0-6

www.spaghettionmondays.com
 Become our fan on Facebook: SpaghettiOnMondays

For Mom and Dad…

...and Steve, Marie, Vince (Carter), Kathy, Robert, Jim, John, Stephanie (Moomer), and Tony.

And to all the great neighbors in our little corner of Iron Mountain, Michigan, who made living there such a memorable experience.

Especially Jack and Mary Rahoi (God rest their souls) and Mark and Mike Ellingson. We can't thank them enough for all they did for us.

Acknowledgments

I'd like to thank Georganna Hancock and Bonita Kale for their great editing and Elizabeth Russell for her legal advice.

I'd also like to thank retired Iron Mountain High School English teachers Ann Markell and Dixie Brown for reviewing the final manuscript and providing very helpful comments and suggestions.

Any grammar or style errors in this book are my responsibility. I sacrificed several suggested corrections in the name of "comedic presentation."

The following stories are true. Some of the names, not so much.

"No one can go through life without eating a baked potato." Barb Flaminio, *circa* 1978

Contents

How Many Sets of Twins?

"I just delivered that woman's fourth set of twins," said a teary-eyed Dr. Klingler to a nurse outside a delivery room at Dickinson County Memorial Hospital in Iron Mountain, Michigan. It was January 10, 1970, and Mom had just given birth to Tony and Stephanie, her ninth and tenth (and last) children. I was now a big brother to seven children and a little brother to two.

After the birth of her third set of twins (Jim and John) in 1969, Mom told Dr. Klingler she wanted to go on the pill. Sometimes, economic reality trumps Papal directives. He told her she didn't need the pill; an intrauterine device (IUD) would be good enough. Well, apparently IUD also stands for "It Uh, Didn't work." The contraceptive failure didn't lead to litigation, but it did lead to ligation.

Mom stayed in the hospital for a few days after the birth, we were told, to have her appendix removed. Perplexed, we all had the same question, "What's an appendix?"

Years later, we found out the real reason for the extended stay was that Dr. Klingler tied Mom's tubes right after the birth; I'm assuming with her permission. Talk about not wasting any time — "Barb, since you're already here." Mom got her tubes tied and sentenced to life with no possibility of parole. It's like in the 1980s when they pulled Baby Jessica from that well in Texas; I'm sure they sealed it up right away to avoid another mishap. It was the same for Mom because whenever Dad went to the well, there was a good chance nine months later there would be a bucket of kids. Mom thinks Dr. Klingler had some guilt over his birth control recommendation because there was no hospital bill for the delivery and "appendectomy."

When Tony and Stephanie came home, their fingers were so tiny and dainty; I was afraid to touch them because I thought they'd break. Their tied-off umbilical cords looked like gray macaroni to me, but after a few days, they dried up and fell off.

A few months later, they were baptized. Not in a church, but in our kitchen, right in front of the refrigerator. And this was a Catholic baptism by a priest. Our kitchen was where we washed dirty dishes and original sin. Sinless and Kenmore. I wonder at how many christenings someone said, "Just a minute, Father, I have to take the buns out of the oven."

The priest placed a ceremonial white cloth on the kitchen table and set candles on top. Mom probably looked at the cloth and started sizing diaper cuts. When Father pulled up the cloth afterwards, chances are it was stuck to the table on some drying grape jelly.

Uncle Sonny and Grandma Hazus were Tony and Stephanie's godparents, one set for both of them. This was one of those times when the godparent count was limited by kitchen square footage. Uncle Sonny held Tony, and Grandma Hazus held Stephanie during the ceremony. Uncle Sonny wore a dark yellow cardigan sweater that was the same shade as the refrigerator. Grandma wore a powder blue dress, the same color as one of her Cadillacs.

Father finished in record time at the Amana from Heaven altar. First Tony, then Stephanie. Lather, rinse, and repeat. No Catholic Mass, just a quick rejection of Satan. The priest told us he was going snowmobiling after the baptism. That seemed odd, a priest snowmobiling. Surely he was a priest, wasn't he? Baptize babies in a kitchen, snowmobiling afterwards, just like they tell them in the seminary. I wonder if he'd be frolicking in the snow with other men of the kitchen cloth — "You'll never guess where I just performed a baptism. Seriously, take a guess."

~~~

Mom had six pregnancies and ten kids from 1962 to 1970. Steve and Marie in February 1962, me in January 1963, and Vince and Kathy in October 1963. What!? No, the 1963 births weren't a time-delay triplet birth. Vince and Kathy were born a few months premature; that's why the math doesn't add up. Robert arrived in November 1964, and the fertility gods granted mercy for a few years before she had another set of twins in February 1969 (Jim and John), followed by Tony and Stephanie in January 1970. That's makes seven out of ten of us with a birthday in January or February. Astrologists might have something to say about that — maybe that Mom and Dad got tipsy on wine in April or May and one thing led to another. There were two other Italian families in our neighborhood with six kids each. I think our neighborhood is in the Opus Dei Hall of Fame.

Ten kids may have made Mom long for the carefree days when she had only (only!) six in a two-and-a-half year span by the time she was twenty-three years old. During our first winter in Iron Mountain, Dad was working the night shift at a tool manufacturer, so one night Mom took us for a sled ride down the alley. She found a sled big enough for six kids. Maybe it was a toboggan. I know it wasn't Rosebud. None of us had winter boots, so she just put bread bags over our regular shoes. They were probably Holsum bread bags; that's the brand we ate. Apparently, at Holsum they were into bread baking and not spelling bees. The Food and Drug Administration didn't require ingredient labels on food in the 1960s, but I'm sure Holsum made their bread with yeest and flowr. With six kids to feed and living on a shoestring budget, boots weren't as important as what used to be in those bags. Maybe our feet weren't toasty, but at least they were dry.

So off we went for some Holsum family fun: two five-year-olds, a four-year-old, two three-year-olds and a two-year-old, with Mom pulling the rope attached to the sled. I wonder how many twenty-three-year-old women could accomplish that feat today (not including Amish women)? That spiritual song, "Swing Low, Sweet Chariot" probably would have been appropriate about then. She hadn't realized how hard it would be to pull six of us on that sled. About three blocks down the alley, she was in tears. She turned around and struggled to get her Donner Party back home. Did she ever think in her wildest dreams that she would need a ten-kid sled for the same trip a few years later?

So there you have it, a family of twelve— two parents, two singles, and four sets of twins from an Italian father and a Ukrainian/Lithuanian mother. I always thought growing up in Iron Mountain in the 1970s was pretty average, nothing spectacular. Another school year went by and then it was summer with its fun activities—a little mischief here and there, but nothing warranting police action. However, as we got older and recounted the stories from our childhood, I realized we lived a vibrant life on Hughitt Street. With that many people stacked in one house, how couldn't we? No, it wasn't perfect, but it sure was colorful.

Mom and the other ladies in the neighborhood had weekly coffee gabfests. Those were the days when a man's income could support a family and the women were free to get together to discuss the pressing issues of the day over large doses of caffeine and a cloud of nicotine. I remember one gathering when Mom told her friends a funny story about our family. "You should write a book!" said one of the ladies after gulping down a Marlboro/Maxwell House speedball. Thirty some years later, I took her up on it.

These stories follow no particular order, but according to Einstein, it doesn't matter. He once said, "The distinction between past, present and future is only a stubbornly persistent illusion." If Einstein says the march of time is an illusion, it's good enough for me.

An American Werewolf in the Coal Bin

Our home on the corner of Hughitt and Maple Streets was an early 1900s two-story house with white clapboard siding. The house had an extension, like a big shed with a single-slope roof. The top of the roof butted against the upstairs bedroom windows, and sometimes we'd push up a window sash, climb through, and perch on the roof, rotating our heads and scanning the neighborhood. We looked like squatting gargoyles guarding the temple.

The low end of the shed roof was only about seven feet from the ground, so it wasn't like we could parachute off it. I know that for a fact. One day I got the bright idea to float down to the ground, so I climbed up on the roof with an umbrella and jumped off. Geronimo! Two sore ankles later, I figured instead of imitating Mary Poppins, I should just stick to doing the Morton Salt Girl.

The basement was sandstone and mortar, typical of old houses in Upper Michigan. Most of the basement beneath the extension was unfinished, except for the walkway to the real basement. A big opening next to the walkway looked like a cave; we stored scrap wood and junk in there. We were all afraid to walk by it because there was no telling what nocturnal creature dwelled in there. When we finally cleaned it out, we found a dehydrated rat looking like furry jerky. The rat's cousin had crawled up into our still-warm car engine one cold November night for a good night's sleep. When Dad started the car the next morning, he murdered the rat, pinching it in an engine belt. Flip a coin for which screeched louder. The rat was in one of those hard to reach places that tick off mechanics, so Dad taped a jack knife to a stick and sawed it in half with the skill of a stage magician. This was no illusion though. Part of it dropped to the ground, its better half whipsawed out when Dad started the car.

A coal-fired furnace in the basement heated our house. The coal bin, a small room about eight feet long and four feet wide, was near the furnace. The coal was black and shiny and shaped like potatoes. There was an old saying, "If you're not good, you'll get a lump of coal in your stocking for Christmas." If we were bad, Mom and Dad didn't have far to go for stocking stuffers.

Our coal was delivered by a truck that was loaded at a downtown rail terminal, behind the Kentucky Fried Chicken. This was back when there was no shame in the word "fried," and they didn't deploy "KFC" as a sleight-of-hand marketing maneuver. Propped high on a pole was one of those huge spinning chicken buckets with Colonel Sanders' face on it. The Orwellian Colonel, with his 360-degree view of Iron Mountain, kept a watchful eye on its citizens. We all wished that one day we could go for a ride in that bucket. Most kids in America dreamed about going to Disney World or a Six Flags amusement park; we dreamed about going for a ride in a spinning chicken bucket. Is that so different from a ride in a spinning teacup?

The coal was stored in two large silos at the terminal; the trucks backed up to them to get a load dumped in. I don't think being the daughter of a coal driver in Iron Mountain lead to any careers in country music. Our coal delivery man, Joe Badini (Joe the Coal Man to us), backed his truck onto our yard from Maple Street and parked in front of the little steel door cut in the basement wall below the kitchen window. We'd line up in the window to watch, and

Joe always smiled and waved at the row of little heads. After he lowered a metal chute from the truck bed through the bin opening, he'd stand on the truck's passenger side and pull a lever, slowly tilting the bed. Gravity took over and shiny black spuds cascaded down the slide, shaking the whole house as they slammed onto the concrete floor. We could really feel the rumble since our ringside seats were right over the coal bin. We liked it so much we almost forgot about the chicken bucket rides.

The coal was shoveled out of the bin and carried to the furnace. I have no idea if it was bituminous or anthracite coal; all I know is it kept the house nice and cozy. The furnace had a small opening in the front with a tiny steel door; it looked like an Industrial Revolution contraption that kept kids busy at the turn of the century. Mom started the fire with balled-up newspaper and a few chunks of coal. Once kindled, she tossed in more black carbon to stoke the fire. I can still picture Mom, scooping up coal in the bin, walking to the furnace, tossing it into the raging fires, and then walking back to reload. Imagine raising ten kids and loading coal into a furnace with a shovel. If Charles Dickens wrote that, you'd call him a liar.

When you'd thrust the shovel into the coal pile, it made the muffled sound of a metal blade slicing through chunks of coal. Chook. Chook. Chook. It's the same sound that would feed my head when it rested on a pillow at bedtime, as blood pulsed through my inner ear. Every time I heard that bloody cadence, my mind conjured up a frightful coal bin scene — a werewolf in striped pajamas slicing a spade into that pile of Kentucky State Rock, the shoveling synchronized with the sound in my head. Chook-werewolf shovel, chook-werewolf shovel, chook-werewolf shovel. Why a werewolf in striped pajamas? Because Frankenstein in striped pajamas looks ridiculous. We finally got a natural gas furnace in the mid 1970s. No more coal pile and no more werewolves. The natural gas furnace didn't make any noise. I'm surprised I didn't imagine a mime in the basement.

After we got the gas furnace, the coal bin became a storage room.

Mom and Dad "hid" our Christmas presents in there. They'd place them in the back, cover them with a blanket and then push a few things in front to try to trick us, but it never worked. We always found them. From stocking stuffer inventory to Christmas present storage, the room still served its holiday purpose.

Mom did a lot of dirty, sweaty chores in the basement; there was no time for pampering down there. Although disposable diapers were a consumer staple in the 1970s, as far as Mom was concerned cotton was king, so she still put cloth diapers on the fruit of her womb. It's not because Mom was a green movement pioneer; however the diapers were involved in some green movements. Cloth diapers were an economic necessity. The family budget could absorb the cost of reusable cloth more than of disposables.

She wouldn't just go to JC Penney's and buy them off the shelf; creative frugality was required, and I don't doubt Mom made them out of random bolts of cloth. No, she didn't use burlap bags; all of our diapers were cotton (or a texturally similar synthetic substitute). Although I doubt the fiber count in our diapers matched that of the bed linen at The Drake in Chicago, I don't think it would have been too far-fetched to see a "Holiday Inn" stamp on one of our diapers.

Just about every day, Mom had to face the unpleasant task of diaper cleaning, and as with everything else, she was up to the challenge. Good thing, too, because no one else was. Maybe the werewolf helped shoveling coal, but he wouldn't go near a dirty diaper. Maytag repairman, hell, *this* was the loneliest job in the world. Even undocumented workers today would probably turn it down. I know our nanny hated it. Oh, that's right; my pretend family had the nanny.

You had to (or I should say Mom had to) empty the diapers and then get to work. She washed them in a metal tub with an old-fashioned corrugated, tin-plate washboard. She held the board upright in the tub filled with soapy water and scrubbed the diapers up and down over the board, again and again, slaving over the soiled cotton. This is the type of mess that no detergent's TV commercial would dare say it could remove. Mom wasn't impressed how a Proctor and Gamble soap could remove a red wine stain from a blouse. Tide or Cheer, in the end did it really matter? And let's be honest, a detergent named Cheer in this situation is a cruel joke.

So Mom shoveled coal into a furnace and washed dirty diapers on a tin washboard in a dark, stone basement. It was like a turn of the century laundry convent in Ireland where they sent "wayward" young women to do penance for their sins with some soul-cleansing labor.

~~~

Every year, barn swallows nested below the eaves on the Maple Street side of the house. Those little birds with the blue-black wings and white underbellies looked like little penguins, and they were swift as heck. During nesting season, they dived at us like kamikaze pilots, so we threw rocks or apples at them. Target practice with live swallows was a lot more fun than with clay pigeons. We never nailed one, but a few times, we hit the house across Maple Street.

Those swallows would spit out little balls of mud, forming an enclosed nest with a round opening just large enough to squeeze in. There'd usually be about five or six nests in a row with those little swallow heads poking out, taunting us. We tried hosing down the nests when they started building them, but that never seemed to work. They'd be right back at it and work non-stop all day, fixing and building. They must have come from Mexico every spring.

Mom read somewhere or someone told her that swallows are afraid of owls, so we tested that theory. We bought a plastic owl about a foot tall and four inches wide and hung it on our house beside the nesting area. I know real owls aren't made of plastic and are larger than one foot tall. Apparently, swallows know that too. To top it off, it looked more like a cartoon owl than a real one. It kind of reminded me of a bubble bath container — other kid's bubble baths, not ours. (If it were ours, we would have hung an empty Palmolive dish soap bottle up there.) I wonder what swallow laughter sounds like. Plastic owls — like a terrible sequel to *The Graduate* when Dustin Hoffman's character starts a doomed business based on career advice that guy offered at his graduation party. I wonder how many people drove by our house, looked at that owl, and said "What the...?" At some point, I think we realized how ridiculous a plastic owl looked tacked to our house and we took it down. The owl, not the house; we needed the house.

Upstairs were four bedrooms. When we numbered only eight, there was one for each pair: Mom and Dad, Marie and Kathy, Vince and Robert, Steve and I. We were Feng Shui masters and didn't even know it.

When we first moved to Iron Mountain, we'd sometimes leave our bedrooms early in the morning and flop on Mom and Dad's bedroom floor, like a pack of wolves. No disputing who the alpha male was. One morning in the flop house I got up to move and Marie's head was in the way. I almost tripped on it and said, "Marie move or I'll step on your f***ing head."

Uh oh. Dad wasn't sleeping because he bolted right up, pointed his finger at me and said "Where did you hear that word?"

Time for quick thinking— the proper response may get me out of this mess; the wrong one could mean trouble, and I don't mean Dad would have pulled out Hasbro's pop-o-matic game Trouble. I quickly gathered my thoughts and blurted out the first thing that came to mind.

"On 'Bozo'," I said.

"Where did you hear it?" my Dad asked again incredulously.

"On 'Bozo'," I pleaded.

I told my Dad I heard the F-bomb on the *Bozo the Clown* television show. I'm sure Bozo never dropped an "effer" on his show, but for some reason, I told Dad that's where I'd heard it. Dad let it go at that and lay back down. Maybe he was laughing. I hope he was thinking "Not bad, kid. Not bad." I always wondered where I heard that word. Probably from an older kid in the neighborhood.

~~~

A little window at the end of the upstairs hallway landing looked out to the western sky. The 1970s were the time for "crazes," like unidentified flying objects (UFOs) and streaking (running around naked in public). A streaker usually popped up at a sporting event or on a televised program. Someone streaked at the Academy Awards in 1974, running behind actor David Niven when he stood at the podium. A streaker also ran onto the green during a professional golf tournament, only to be blindsided by golfer Peter Jacobsen's textbook-form tackle. I always wondered when someone went streaking at a nudist colony if he was fully clothed.

At night, if I had to go downstairs, I didn't like looking out that window because I thought I might see a UFO. As if aliens in a UFO hovering in the sky would shine a beam into that little window and abduct me Patty Hearst-style. However, I never feared looking out the window and seeing streakers.

As is typical of old houses, the hallway was very narrow. I found out that barefoot I could put my right foot and hand on one wall and my left foot and hand on the opposite wall and crawl up to the ceiling, just like Spiderman. I'd wedge myself up there, lying in wait to scare one of siblings when they got to the top of the stairs. Plus, if I ever saw a UFO out the window, I had my own little panic room. I could scurry up the walls to the ceiling and hide, safe from alien medical experiments.

The Exorcist movie was released in 1973, and although we were all too young to see it, everyone talked about it and it was in the news, so we knew about the possessed little girl with the spinning head. Now I developed a devil and demon anxiety. (The devil piloting a flying saucer probably would have given me a heart attack.) I started saying an "Our Father" and a "Hail Mary" in bed every night to hedge my bets against demonic possession. I guess you could call me an opportunistic Catholic. When I went downstairs in the dark, I'd sprint waving my hand behind my back to make sure none of Lucifer's legionnaires were on my tail.

You'd think I would have fallen, but it was Kathy who fell on the stairs. But not going down. She was the only person I knew who could fall up. You'd hear the clump-clump of feet going up and then "Ba da boom!" "Kathy," we'd say with a shrug. If she had said an "Our Father" before going to bed at night, maybe that demon wouldn't have tripped her all the time.

Old houses have very small bathrooms, just large enough for a toilet, sink, and bathtub. A bathroom in the old days was called a water closet and the name was true to form. You took care of business and got out of there. Bathroom math used to be about number one and number two. Now it's about square footage and fractions of baths.

Our bathtub was right below the stairs, so the ceiling above the tub was the slanted contour of the stairway, taking up space in already cramped quarters. A clothes hamper for a family our size wasn't practical. There were a few feet of space between the bathtub end and the wall, so Dad figured it would be a good place to make a laundry chute to the basement. Maybe Joe the Coalman's delivery system inspired him. Dad cut a hole in the floor and nailed in a short piece of wood paneling, slanting it like a slide. We called it "the chute." In our bathroom, we played chutes and bladders. The dirty laundry target was a big wooden box in the basement. When you were down there, it was funny seeing underwear do a six-foot free fall into the box.

In theory, every time we tossed a shirt or pair of pants in the chute, it would slide straight into the box. That would have been so if we wore silk kimonos. In reality, a pair of bell-bottom jeans might not slide down. Then someone would toss another pair on top, repeated several times a day, and before you knew it, there was a laundry logjam. When the pile looked like procrastination at a Chinese laundry, one of us would foot-stomp it to force the clothes down. Drains weren't the only things we had to unclog in our bathroom.

Sometimes, the box in the basement went AWOL under a huge pile of dirty clothes, another friendly reminder to Mom she had yet another household task. If clean laundry was scarce, you could always go over to the pile for wardrobe selection. Rule of thumb, top of the pile OK, middle to bottom, forget it. Just pluck something off the top and give it the sniff test. If it didn't smell too bad, we were in business. I believe in accounting this is known as the LIFO method of inventory control – last in, first out. That shirt would find its way back in a few days anyway.

After a few years, Mom and Dad moved their bedroom into the house extension, next to the kitchen. They were probably worried we'd hear typical noises that come from the bedroom of a married couple, like dice shaking in a cup and someone yelling "Yahtzee!" A little shuttered window in the kitchen opened into their bedroom. That came in handy when Dad was in bed, and we were making a lot of morning noise. The shutters would open and his head would pop out; he'd tell us to knock it off, and then they'd close just as fast — a sideways jack-in-the-box. He was like one of those jokesters on *Rowan and Martin's Laugh In*, a 1970s sketch comedy show. A little door in the wall opened, a head popped out and told a joke, the audience laughed, the head retreated and the door closed. Dad's comedic timing wasn't as good as that from those prairie dog comedians.

~~~

When I was around six years old, Steve and I had a pillow fight in our bedroom. We had spongy foam rubber pillows and after belting each other for a while, we thought it would be funny to pick off pieces of foam and stick them in our noses. Other kids played games or kick ball for fun; we shoved things in our noses. We restarted the pillow fight with foam boogers hanging out of our nostrils. I think we were trying to see if we could whack them out of each other's nose. We wore out quickly, probably from oxygen deficiency, so we called it a draw and took out our nose plugs.

A few days later, Steve developed bad breath, so Mom made him brush his teeth a lot and use mouthwash. It didn't help; his breath still smelled like rancid meat. We finally told Mom about our nostril plug pillow fight, and she figured that a piece of foam had lodged up Steve's nose and was festering in the dark, moist nasal cavity. Apparently, Steve didn't have any difficulty breathing; at least he didn't say so. Maybe he just thought he had a cold and toughed it out, a go-to remedy in our house.

Mom usually diagnosed ailments in our family as "gas." Mom, my stomach hurts; It's gas. Mom, I got a headache; It's probably gas. Mom, what's this growth on my cheek; Oh, it's just gas. If a malady in our house didn't involve blood pouring from a wound, then in Mom's book, it was probably just abdominal methane.

Dr. Klinger was a great family doctor, and gave us favorable health-care payment terms, but nasal blockage would have wasted his time, so Mom set up the kitchen emergency room for Steve's nose job. From baptisms to minor surgery, our kitchen was truly a multi-functional space. Mom sat on a chair, assisted by her sister Denise, visiting from Pennsylvania. Steve stood in front of Mom, and she tilted his head back to take a look. That dark cavern held its secrets. She plopped a cigarette in her mouth and nervously fumbled a match trying to light it. This was her first operation as the resident physician, so her nerves could be excused. Steve got scared once he saw Mom light the match. He thought she was going to stick the match up his nose for illumination, or even worse try to scorch the foam to extinction. His fears were unfounded; she just lit the cigarette and inhaled some cool menthol relief. Those were the days when you didn't have to walk outside your own house to have a smoke. Second-hand smoke? Are you kidding? Heck, some doctors even smoked in their offices.

Mom slowly inserted the tweezers up Steve's nose. Luckily, his nostrils were wide enough that she didn't need a retractor. She was sweating like a bomb defuser, trying to guess which color wire to cut. She got the tweezers up there pretty far and hit pay dirt. Once she pulled out that days-old piece of spongy foam, it was obvious why Steve had dragon breath. She tweezered it out just like in the game "Operation" that was popular in the 1970s. Mom must not have hit the sides of Steve nose because the buzzer didn't go off.

Steve was a health insurance claimant more than any of us, usually for head trauma. One afternoon after school, he ran around the house for the stadium across the street. There was a puny pine tree in our front yard that we always hurdled. During this steeplechase, there was a rubber ball on the ground behind the tree and Steve's landing foot hit dead center on the spongy orb. His feet flew out beneath him, and his face raced toward the ground, his body's torque complementing the earth's gravity. A firm landing on the turf would have allowed him to save face. Unfortunately, his head's trajectory terminated at a cinder block, his forehead slamming on the block's edge. It was just like a Roadrunner and Wiley E. Coyote routine. I think the ball and the cinder block both had "ACME" written on them. An emergency room visit and some stitches were his consolation prize.

One summer afternoon, Steve and Mark Tedeschi were picking blueberries outside the City Park when some kid rode up on his bike and started mouthing off. Like in a debate, Mark offered a profanity-laced counterpoint. As Steve was bending down picking blueberries and shoveling them in his mouth, the sound of "spuck" echoed through the pines. That kid had hurled a rock, scoring a bullseye on Steve's frontal lobe. After the initial shock wore off, Steve and his friend sprinted after him. While the Goliath Steve was chasing after David, he felt fluid oozing down his face, so he wiped his face with his hand and gazed at his blood-soaked palm. Steve yelled, "Hey kid, I'm bleeding." The knuckleballer must have felt guilty because he came back, took off his tee shirt and pressed it on Steve's wound. They all jumped on their bikes and went into the park. That kid's Mom was there, so they went to her for some maternal wisdom. Steve didn't tell her that her little angel was the culprit. He just wanted to get home. The woman drove Steve home, hoping Mom would be there.

A little while later I came home. Mom wasn't home, and Mark

was sitting on our porch steps outside, and he told me what had happened. I ran inside and saw Steve sitting in a chair at the kitchen table. His head was tilted back, and the kid's Mom was dragging on a cigarette, pressing a wet cloth against his forehead. First aid in our kitchen had to be administered under the influence of nicotine. She said the cut was bad and lifted the cloth to show me. It was so deep, you could see his skull. I'll never forget how lily white the bone looked contrasted against the glistening, red head meat. Mom soon showed up and took Steve to the hospital for some catgut sutures.

In our family, there was never a follow-up visit to Dr. Klingler to remove stitches. Since it was just snipping and pulling out thread, it was in Mom's wheelhouse. It's the same as altering a hemline, but instead of polyester, it's an epidermal layer. No big deal. Tony (the youngest twin) had a few stitches near his temple when he was a toddler. After Mom concluded his Frankenstein embroidery was in long enough, she waited until he was asleep and using her scissors, removed the thread with the skill of an Asian sweatshop seamstress.

We had other medical emergencies in our house. We had some radio tubes on our front porch — little glass, vacuum-sealed bulbs that kind of look like clear Christmas tree lights. Why we had them, who knows. John must have confused them with candy because he bit into one. Mom was worried that John may have swallowed some of the powdery material in the tube, so she called Dr. Klingler's office.

"This is Barb Flaminio and believe it or not, my son bit into a radio tube." That must have been when the secretary handed the phone to a nurse because Mom said again, "This is Barb Flaminio and believe it or not, my son bit into a radio tube."

She must have finally reached Dr. Klingler because she had to repeat it one more time. There was no trip to the doctor. I think he just told Mom to have John open his mouth, rotate his head, and see if he picks up any stations.

Good to the Last Drop

Early one morning, Mom and Dad were in the kitchen eating breakfast when they heard someone banging on the side porch door screaming, "Let me in! Let me in!" Mom and Dad knew it was too early and too aggressive for Mormons, so it couldn't be good. It was an escapee from psychiatric care at the hospital, wrapped in a rug he had taken from someone else's porch. Dad told him to get lost, or maybe more like, "Get the hell out of here!" I'm surprised Mom didn't shout, "And leave the rug." We could always use more of those. The guy got the hint and scurried around the house. Unfortunately, our porch didn't have any wardrobe accessories for him; a window curtain for a shawl would have really tied his outfit together.

The police were on his tail and showed up at our house a few minutes later asking Dad if he saw some crazy rug-draped guy. Dad told them the Berber bandit was just at our house and, "He went that-a-way." The cops followed his trail and soon ended his magic carpet ride. If Dad had let him inside to hang around for a while, he probably would have run back voluntarily to the hospital.

Like Colombian kids, we loved coffee at breakfast. Most of us took our first hit by kindergarten. If anything a house full of ten kids needs, it's ten kids jacked up on caffeine. "More coffee?" is what you'd expect a woman to say to her husband at breakfast, not her five year old kid. Sure Mom, but only half a cup, we're going to be coloring today and I want to stay in the lines.

We had a metal percolating coffee pot, like all caffeine addicts. Joe DiMaggio wasn't hawking drip coffee makers yet. When I was around six years old, I was pouring piping hot coffee into my cup and spilled it on my wrist. This was a regular "big people" cup, not one of those sippy cups. And there were no little sissified coffee cups with saucers in our house either. I let out a "yelp" and Mom wrapped my wrist with cotton gauze. A good placebo effect. I don't remember if Mom had a menthol vapor stick dangling from her mouth during the first aid. I went to school with my bandaged wrist. Surprisingly, my teacher didn't ask me about it:

"What happened to your wrist?"

"I burned it."

"You burned it? How?"

"Uh, spilled my coffee."

"Seriously, what happened? You can tell me. Hold this stuffed animal."

More important than our caffeine fix was our sugar fix, courtesy of the barons of Battle Creek. We loved cereal; our breakfasts were always cereal, toast, and coffee. We ate the monster cereals—Count Chocula, Frankenberry, and Booberry. I was disappointed there was no Werewolf cereal. We liked Cap'n Crunch, Quisp, and Quake too. On the Quake box was a hard hat-wearing miner who probably would have failed a steroid test. Quisp had a cheerful alien with a propeller on a stick coming out of his head. If that was what aliens were really like, I'd have no problem looking out the upstairs window at night. Quisp was shaped like little saucers and Quake was little gears. Cap'n Crunch really sweetened the pot when they came out with Cap'n Crunch with Crunchberries. Those were just little red balls of sugar and I didn't like them because they'd scrape the roof of my mouth.

These cereals were typical 1970s sugar-loaded goodies. If you'd polled five dentists, I'd bet not one would have recommended these cereals to their patients. That lone holdout in the sugarless gum survey could not, in good conscience, disagree with his colleagues again.

When we were just a family of eight, there was one chair for each of us around the kitchen table. After we became twelve, Dad made two benches for the ten kids, though there were no seat numbers on them like at a stadium. We were the second and third string basketball players, waiting for the coach to put us in the game. Dad built a shelf beneath each bench seat for cereal box storage. The boxes took up every inch of space on the shelving; there was no extra room for baptismal supplies. The only chairs at the table were at each end, for the King and Queen.

Every breakfast, we'd each chomp, smack, and slurp a bowl of cereal with the cereal box about two-inches from our faces, engrossed in reading and oblivious to our fellow coffee mates. As they always say, "Turn off the television and read," although I don't think they mean reading material from General Mills. We were all surprised the first time we went to a library and didn't find cereal boxes to read. We could have done our grade school book reports based on the back of a box: In some far away land there's this bird that says he's cuckoo for Cocoa Puffs...

Cereal boxes usually came with cheap prizes inside; and, of course, it was always at the bottom, but as it says on the box, "Contents may settle during shipping." Maybe we were supposed to wait until we ate our way down to the prize. Like we were going to do that. We just burrowed our hands into the cereal to get what was always a cheap toy, like that ridiculous "rock ball" in the Cocoa Pebbles. The rock ball was a hollow plastic ball the size of a golf ball; it had bumps and ridges, so it looked like a rock, and it didn't bounce a lick. I don't think they cared in the cigar smoke-filled boardrooms in Battle Creek.

Before bedtime, we'd usually clamor for one last bowl of cereal.

They say reading a book before bed is a good way to get sleepy. I guess the back of a cereal box is a reasonable substitute. By this time, Mom was usually on the couch fighting off the sand man, exhausted from a day of running a house full of ten kids and getting ready to do it all again the next day. We'd usually hit her up for that last bowl when her defenses were weakest, right before she nodded off to la-la land. Four or five times a night, "Mom, can I have a bowl of cereal?" echoed from the living room.

Mom did the grocery shopping and was in charge of the food budget; she knew the cereal had to last until the next grocery store excursion. But she'd usually give in with a compromise of "half a bowl." That was our chance to defy parental authority, because we could take at least three-quarters of a bowl. If we were feeling daring, a full bowl.

My younger brother Jim became tired of his sounding like a broken record every night asking for one last bowl, so one time he cabled his request. He folded his telegraph that requested a bowl of cereal into a paper airplane and floated it to Mom, who was lying on the couch anticipating the serial requests for a bedtime snack. It was a perfect landing but an unsuccessful kamikaze attack. Mom was fast asleep, and the plane just rested on the flight deck.

In the 1970s, in our town, milk came in glass bottles or cartons left on the front porch by the milkman. Looking back, it seems strange. Now, you just go to a store or a gas station and pick up a gallon of milk with a lottery ticket. The dairy producers must have convinced America that only highly specialized milk truck drivers could handle this dangerous task. They weren't trucks either, they were white vans without a passenger seat, so the driver could grab the milk and bolt to the porch.

We didn't have whole milk; we had Mom's hybrid concoction. Because the family budget had to stretch more than a Hollywood face, Mom "cut" the milk. Half-and-half to most people means half milk and half cream. People at the Waldorf-Astoria maybe. For us, half-and-half was Mom's golden ratio of half whole milk and half instant. In those days, all milk was whole, the other part of the equation was instant powdered milk from a box. As kids, we thought milk came from cows and boxes. You'd just add water to the powder to make "milk," and apparently, it was cheaper than the real thing. I don't know how, since they took real milk (I think), dehydrated it, and made a powder that you'd add to water to turn it back into milk. Why not cut out the middleman and just keep it liquid? When Mom made the instant lactose in a pitcher, it formed a big foam head on the top, like beer poured from a tap. She'd mix the real and instant in "equal parts" and voila, – half-and-half. Thinking back, I question Mom's math because I believe it was really 30-70 milk. I think she was skimming our half-and-half. Let's see, if we have half a bowl of cereal and use half-and-half milk, does that mean we are only getting one-fourth of the recommended daily allowance of vitamins and iron?

Crumpets and Cocoa

Dad was born in the neighboring town, Kingsford, in 1940 to Art and Lauretta Flaminio. Mom was born in 1942 in Brooklyn, New York, to Francis (Frank) and Ann Hazus. Dad was seventeen years old when he walked off the stage with his high school diploma and onto a bus to Air Force basic training at Lackland Air Force Base near San Antonio, Texas.

Like a lot of kids in Iron Mountain and Kingsford in the 1950s, he was a good Catholic boy who never missed a Sunday Mass. He liked to brag how even when he was in Basic Training, he'd go to church every Sunday, even though it was his only free day. If Basic Training meant churchgoing for Dad, by the '70s or '80s it was obvious he wasn't in Basic Training anymore. Being a good Catholic boy doesn't necessarily equate to consistent church attendance as an adult. However, I know there's a Book of Job in the Bible, and maybe it says men who work an extra job on Sunday to put food on the table and a roof over the heads of ten kids are exempt from Sunday Mass. Even though I was Catholic, I didn't read the Bible, so I'm assuming that's what the Job program in the Good Book is all about.

Dad had other tales of death-defying church attendance. One Sunday morning when he was fourteen, he and some of his friends took a bus to Milwaukee for a Braves baseball game. These days, I don't think fourteen-year-olds take unescorted two-hundred-mile bus trips to big cities. Plane rides yes, but bus trips, I doubt. Back then, a cross-country bus ride wasn't nearly the adventure it is today. You didn't have to step on Cheetos and scratch-off lottery tickets to get to your seat. Dad said when he and his friends got off the bus late in the morning, the first thing they did was look for a church to attend Mass. Probably after they bummed some smokes off the bus driver.

Mom and Dad met in London, England, where Dad was stationed at the U.S. Air Force Base in South Ruislip, at the west end of the city. Mom's Dad, Grandpa Hazus, was a civilian mortician for the U.S. Air Force in England. When we'd ask Dad how he met Mom, he'd tell us she came up to him in a bar in London and said, "Hey Mac, you wanna' drive my truck?" He'd say that line in a deep gravelly voice; it always cracked us up. Dad served four years, and then re-upped for another four-year term, making sergeant. He has a bunch of moles and spots all over his back; it's peppered with brown and red marks. He looks like Dick Cheney's hunting partner. I used to joke with him that those were bullet scars from Charlie the Viet Cong he fought during his service.

Mom was fortunate to have seen lot of Europe when she was growing up because her Dad worked at different overseas American bases. She remembers late 1940s Germany with huge piles of rubble from Allied bombings still in the city streets. When we watched TV and scenes of London, Paris, or Frankfurt came on, she would say, "I was there! I was there!" She'd gone from cavorting around the Eiffel Tower and Buckingham Palace to Iron Mountain's famous landmarks: the Cornish Mine Pump and Pine Mountain Ski Jump. With all the Italians in Iron Mountain, she could at least pretend she was in Rome.

During Mom's senior year of high school on an American base in England, the base was closing, and most of the students had already moved, so the class sizes were small. On the bright side, her chances for academic success improved with less competition. This and long hours of studying made Mom the valedictorian of her senior class. A class of two students. I guess the salutatorian thought of himself as the second best student or the worst student, depending on his perspective. I wonder if they dated. If he broke up with her, it would have been hard for him to use the,"I want to see other people" excuse.

Steve and Marie were born in February 1962 in London. I followed in January 1963. Once in the late 1980s during an after-lunch family bull session, we talked about important dates in our history. I said, "Let's see Mom, you were married in August 1961, and Marie and Steve were born in February 1962. That's six months after you were .... What the ...!" It dawned on me that Mom and Dad's wedding was before the standard nine-month "whisper period"; it was one of those matters we never thought about. Physics and calculus in college, piece of cake. Marriage math, a little tougher.

In late 1963, we left England for New Jersey, America, and quality dental care. Dad's next duty station was McGuire Air Force Base, part of the Fort Dix military complex. When we landed at the base, a sergeant from Dad's unit met us. He took one look at a Mom and Dad carrying three babies and said with pity in his voice, "You'll never make it on an airman's pay." Then the sarge said, "Ten-hut" and Dad took that as a challenge and had seven more. Kathy and Vince were born at the base hospital in October 1963, three months premature. They spent several weeks in an incubator.

We lived in a little town called Browns Mills. I remember a summer outing at a lake near our house when I was about four. There were prizes in plastic bags buried in the sand and I dug up a bag with a squirt gun. Being New Jersey, maybe it was a real gun buried by some guy named Carmine. Two girls, I think they were Mom's sisters Denise and Debbie, were standing in knee-deep water, each holding one end of a towel. They'd dip it in the water and pull it up full of little fish like anchovies that flapped around on the towel and sparkled silver in the sunlight. Were they were catching our dinner for the night?

One day when Steve and Marie were toddlers, they wandered away from the house. Mom was pregnant with Kathy and Vince at the time and panicked when she realized they were gone. Instinctively, she ran towards the lake. Maybe she was missing a towel and thought they had gone fishing. She caught them on their leisurely stroll to the beach. Mom thought the trauma from that event led to Kathy and Vince's premature birth.

On another afternoon, Steve, Marie, and I were sitting on the hood of the family car having a good old time when a black kid from the neighborhood rode by on his bike. We chanted, "Chocolate face, chocolate face, chocolate face," and it wasn't because he was messy from a Hershey Bar. This was not that we had grown up in a racist family, far from it. We were just little kids who didn't know any better. Lucky for that kid and unlucky for us, Dad heard it and put an end to it right then and there. That kid could have chanted to us, "Strawberry bottoms, strawberry bottoms, strawberry bottoms."

One day, Mom loaded us into the car to pick up Dad at the base. Dad drove home, and I was in the front passenger seat by Mom when I declared, "I'm going to stand up like the milk man does." When I stood up, the car was moving and the passenger-side door wasn't completely shut. It cracked open, and Dad wasted no time grabbing me by the back of my collar and yanking me back in my seat. He moved so quickly, you might have thought I had declared I was the chocolate milkman.

In New Jersey, we had a chocolate Labrador retriever named Shadow. His face too, well, you know. Shadow didn't come with us when we moved to Iron Mountain. Mom and Dad must have "taken him to a farm where he could run free and live with a nice family."

Robert was the last born in New Jersey, in November 1964. In 1967, America's involvement in Vietnam was escalating and several airmen from Dad's unit were leaving for Southeast Asia. With six kids and eight years of service, Dad decided it was time to call it a career. He didn't want to be stationed in Thailand or Da Nang while his wife and six kids were back in the States.

In October 1967, we moved to Iron Mountain, driving in our gray, white-top Chevy Impala sedan. Dad and Mom sat in front, and six little kids were snugly perched in the back seat. In high school, when Dad had thought about having a girl in his car and a six-pack in the back seat, he probably hadn't had this in mind.

Dad had already bought our house on Hughitt Street for the paltry sum of $8,000 with a low-interest loan from the Veterans Administration, courtesy of eight years of service to Uncle Sam — a taxpayer-funded mortgage, not a popular subject these days. When we arrived at the house Dad's family was in the kitchen waiting for us, cigarette smoke hanging in the air over their card game. A smoky kitchen would be a common sight for the next decade.

Before we moved, Dad had lined up a job with a tool manufacturer in Kingsford. He worked the night shift, and when we woke up in the morning, we'd race to his black lunch box on the kitchen table looking for leftover goodies. My favorite was the unfinished bologna sandwiches on white bread with lettuce. That's what I call the breakfast of champions.

Next year, the post office had two job openings, to be filled by a civil service exam. Mom and Dad knew a job with the postal service would be more stable and secure for a large family, so he took the exam. The Iron Mountain postmaster was Frank Borla, who lived a stone's throw from us on "A" Street. As luck would have it, Mr. Borla was also a good friend of my Dad's father Art, my grandfather. After the exam, two new civil servants were added to the government payroll — Dad and his cousin Dan. Dad always points out, however, that he had the highest score on the test. How many people can say both their parents are valedictorians?

Dad was a letter carrier and faithfully went to work every day for

30 years. Neither rain, nor snow, nor sleet, nor the birth of another set of twins kept Dad from getting people their mail. He made it all that time without any major mishaps. When he first started working for the postal service, he got in an accident at the post office with the Impala, smashing the back window. I remember Dad saying how he had glass in his underwear and how funny we thought it was. Boxers or briefs, I have no idea.

When Dad first started delivering mail, he drove a van, similar to the milk mobile. Later, he drove a Jeep. We thought it was the coolest vehicle in town because the driver's side was on the right, like in England.

We soon outgrew the Impala sedan and upgraded to a golden brown Chevy Impala station wagon. I guess Dad was into brand loyalty. The station wagon was the family car to have in the 1970s before SUVs became popular. You were considered high society if you had a station wagon with "wood paneling" on the side. We weren't quite there yet. Our wagon had a standard transmission with a steering wheel column shift and a floor clutch. When Mom and Dad drove, I'd watch them clutch and shift, making mental notes of the shift pattern, wondering if I'd be able to do it when I got older. We all fit in the station wagon with four of us riding in the rear cargo area. That's what you call a low rider.

One sunny afternoon, Mom took us to Lake Antoine (the locals pronounced it "An-twine,") for some summer fun. It was the same day as a parade in town. When we turned onto the main street, Stephenson Avenue, we wound up right behind the last group— a carload of bare-chested kids in a parade moving two miles an hour. We were sort of the last float. You could imagine the blurb: "Sponsored by your local Chevy dealer, demonstrating how the Impala station wagon fits ten kids with room for beach gear!" Too bad, we didn't have any candy to throw; then again, we would have eaten it all. So we just looked out the window at all the parade watchers, and they stared right back.

Several later growth spurts forced another vehicle upgrade,

and this time we bought an International Harvester Travelall, the precursor to today's SUVs. It wasn't four-wheel drive, but it could comfortably hold a family 12, and had "wood paneling" on the sides. Our Travel All was olive green. There were two others in the neighborhood, one an Uncle Sonny cardigan yellow and one a Grandma Hazus Cadillac powder blue.

One day in the early 1970s, Dad was delivering mail on "A" Street, the next street over. One family on his route had relatives visiting from out of town who'd brought with them a big German shepherd named Condor. That dog was as intimidating as the name sounded. When you went by their house, a massive German shepherd head stared at you through the screen door, eyeing you as if scanning the Serengeti for some succulent gazelle. If Condor really wanted to get outside, I imagine that screen door wasn't going to stop him. Right, Dad?

Dad sauntered up their sidewalk with the mail one day when Condor must have thought, "Tag, you're it" and bolted out the screen door. Before Dad knew it, he was on his back, and the doggy was on top of him, mouth foaming, and teeth gnashing; they were dilated eyeballs to dilated eyeballs. Ironically, they were in the missionary position. Dad was able to thrust his leather mailbag in front of his face. While Condor tore into the bag with his teeth, Dad gave Condor roundhouse punches to the head. That dog just shook them off like Mike Tyson shaking off a Tinkerbell punch.

Dad always had a small spray canister of mace attached to a belt loop, but he didn't have a chance to reach for it. It was a little bigger than a breath spray canister and I'm sure Condor would have just laughed it off — "Is that all you got?"

The guy finally came out of the house and pulled Condor off Dad. (Shouldn't Dad's corner man be the one to throw in the towel?) When he got the dog off, Dad unleashed an expletive rant:

"You keep that f****ing dog off me. I'm not bringing you your f****king mail ever again. F*** you!"

Even Bozo the Clown would have cringed. That guy must have been impressed because the next day he got a post office box.

Raising ten kids on a mailman's salary was tough, so Dad moonlighted as a janitor. Dad was working two jobs, and Mom was shoveling coal and washing dirty diapers on a tin board. Looking back, it's unbelievable what they did to raise their family.

Dad worked nights for Benny's Janitor Service. He usually bumped into the owner Benny McDermott, a Queens, New York, native, when they were in line for lunch at The Pizza Oven. Once when they were queued up smoking cigarettes and waiting for their calzones, Dad asked Benny if he needed any help at night because he was having a tough time making ends meet. Benny said "Hell, yeah," so that was the extent of Dad's janitor job interview. Oral exam only, no written portion like his mailman job required.

For his janitor job, Dad drove a sky blue Volkswagen microbus, one of those hippie mobiles, with "Benny's Janitor Service" plastered on the side in big yellow lettering. The VW had a sliding door on the side and bench seating inside. We loved riding in that thing. Although we weren't quite the "eleven long-haired friends of Jesus in a chartreuse microbus" from the song *Convoy*, we still would have looked right at home in a commune.

One day, Mom told Dad she wanted to take it for a spin, so she hopped in the driver's seat and took off with that cool, sputtering Volkswagen sound. She turned down the alley and did a loop around the block. When she came down Hughitt Street and turned back onto Maple Street, we were in the front yard cheering. We were so happy for her; you would have thought she had just passed her driver's test. Even the swallows poked their heads out of the nests to see what the commotion was all about. It was funny seeing Mom with this big grin on her face, gripping that horizontal steering wheel. Since the engine was in the back of the VW, and the driver's seat was so close to the windshield, it looked like she was driving a Greyhound ("Pick up those Cheetos!"). Hell, she raised ten kids, cooked, cleaned, and shoveled coal, why not drive the bus too?

A few years later, Benny told Dad, "Jimmy, I've had it. I'm moving to Florida. You can have a chunk of my business for $2,000." Benny sold his company name and some of his stops to another guy, but let Dad in on some of the action. Since we needed the janitor income, Dad became a business owner. First though, he had to get a loan from the bank. We didn't have two grand lying around the house. The banker was so impressed that Dad actually had some money in savings (like $100) while raising so many kids, he had no problem giving Dad the loan.

Dad called his business James Flaminio Janitor Service, Inc. Unfortunately, he had to give the VW to the guy who had bought Benny's name. Dad cleaned businesses on Monday, Wednesday, and Thursday nights, and Sunday mornings. Working full time for the postal service and then three nights and a weekend morning, that's what gets you a Sunday Mass free pass. We took turns cleaning with Dad. Mom would go too, as if she didn't have enough to do already. It was quick routine — empty garbage, sweep the floors, and then mop them. We were never more than an hour at one place. When we asked about getting paid, Mom and Dad told us we got housing and meals — that was our pay. You know, you really couldn't argue with that; however, a few years later, Dad would slip Jim and John a dollar when they helped. The younger ones are always spoiled.

During a cleaning run, I had some idle time, so I sat in a vinyl office chair daydreaming and fiddling around. I snooped around the desk and saw an inkpad and stamp. Cool, now I had something to do. I wasn't going to stamp the desk or office furniture, but my body was fair game. I rubbed the stamp into the inkpad and then pressed it up and down the inside both arms, from my wrist up to my scrawny biceps. I looked like a real bad dude with "Paid in Full" all over my arms. This was in the day when only bikers and guys in the military had tattoos, so I had good company. After I finished my stamp collection, I just rested in the chair, counting the seconds until we could leave.

The next morning, the secretary called Mom and asked why one the chairs' arm rests was stamped with ink. She told Mom it looked like some kid did it on purpose. She was right; some kid did purposely stamp some arms. I guess I didn't know that ink on arm skin easily transforms into ink on arm vinyl. I just renamed Dad's business James Flaminio Janitor Service Ink. They told Mom we would have to pay $75 to replace the chair since "we" damaged it. That was probably what they paid Dad for two weeks of cleaning. I thought for sure I would get in trouble, but Dad just shrugged it off. The next time there, he left a check on the desk. That was a lot of money to us, and I felt guilty that my unlicensed tattoo parlor cost us so much. After we'd coughed up the money for the chair, I thought it was ours, but they kept it. I don't know why; we'd paid in full.

Vision Quest

Most of us were born with terrible vision. Myopia, hyperopia, amblyopia, you name it; we were a cornucopia of ocular dysfunction. Vince, Robert, and Kathy had the worst eyesight; all were wearing glasses with thick lenses before learning their A-B-Cs (or by their first hit of coffee). The three are legally blind but don't necessarily like cheese. When they went to the optometrist, and he asked them which way the big E was pointing on the first line of the eye chart, their standard answer was "Wednesday."

Their thick glasses were called "Coke bottles." They looked like the glasses that one Japanese sailor wore in an episode of *Gilligan's Island*. The sailor kind of reminded me of the Viet Cong that may have shot up Dad's back. Vince often repeated one of the sailor's lines from that episode, said when Ginger was coming on to the sailor, getting him excited and fogging his glasses. "You steam grasses," said the amorous seaman. It was a lot funnier when Vince said it with his thick glasses. One of Vince's friends asked him once if his glasses were from Mattel. Knowing Vinny, that was probably the last time the kid asked him that.

Vince and Robert frequently broke the temples off their glasses, so they'd fix them with electrical tape. They always had a thick wad of black tape on one side where the temple connected to the lens frame, and they walked funny because they would list tape-side. We were grateful that our optometrist, Dr. Lorn Johnson, was so lenient with our eye care payment plan. The financial latitude he gave us would make even sleazy sub-prime mortgage lenders cringe. I think we paid cash at the hardware store for the electrical tape.

When we put up our Christmas tree, the siblings with mole-like vision would remove their glasses and stare at the tree lights. Their retinas so mashed the visible spectrum, all they experienced were bright, fuzzy colorful blotches, and marmalade skies. It didn't take much to amuse us. Those of us with proper spherical eye balls borrowed their glasses to go on the same trip down Peyote Parkway.

My vision is only half as bad as theirs is. Literally, one-half. I'm legally blind in my left eye; it has uncorrectable, blurred vision. My left eye muscles are so weak that I have a natural reflex to squeeze the eye shut in sunlight. In a picture of the first six of us at a wedding reception in the late '60s, my left eye is clamped shut. We were all dressed in our Sunday best; the boys in jackets and ties, and Marie and Kathy in nice dresses. Steve was wearing a plaid sports coat and bow tie that both of us had worn for our kindergarten pictures. I think it was from JC Penney's Wink Martindale clothing line. In the picture, there's Steve with his game-show host outfit and his hands in his pockets with an East Coast elitist boarding school smile — "I guess I'll stand for this photo with you heathens this one time. Where's my pipe?"

I know the sun was out when the photo was snapped because I have my typical "eyes in the sun look," like someone had just asked me a perplexing question, and I'm squeezing my left eye shut, tilting my head and saying, "Huh?" A lady in our neighborhood took the picture and gave it to Mom recently.

One winter in the early '70s, this neighbor's teenage kids built a huge snow sculpture of a hand giving the middle finger in their yard. Maybe it was their retort to a neighborly dispute. I guess Florida wasn't the only place with snowbirds that winter.

Those hormone-saturated high schoolers weren't the only snow *artistes* in the neighborhood. A few blocks down "A" Street, Mr. Andreini made a snow sculpture every winter in his front yard of a big "A." I'm guessing it was for his last name and not his street because the street signs had that covered. So for one winter these snow sculptures proudly proclaimed we lived in the "F*****n' A" neighborhood.

~~~

Vince's poor vision didn't cloud his quest for scientific insight. One morning when he was in grade school, he was leaving for school when Mom saw he had something in his hand.

"What do have there?"

"This," Vince said, showing Mom.

"Do you know what that is," Mom asked.

Vince was holding a small, white cardboard tube about three inches long. He explained to Mom that their class was having a special kind of show and tell where you had to put something in a box and a classmate would stick a hand in an opening, feel the object, and guess what it was. Vince told Mom that for the game he was going to bring the telescope in his hand.

"You aren't leaving the house with that," Mom said as she took a tampon applicator away from him. That's what Vince was going to put in his teacher's box. Vinny Galileo, thought he had a telescope! Come to think of it, he wasn't too far off. The lunar cycle and the menstrual cycle are each about twenty-eight days. I don't know what he brought for show and tell after his telescope was confiscated. Maybe one of Dad's "balloons."

Vince was the "tough guy" when we were kids; he was built solid. I didn't tangle with him because I was scrawny. To mimic him, we'd make a menacing face, pull one hand back behind our heads, and cock a fist. I don't think Vince ever actually did that, but in our minds, he'd look funny doing it with his thick glasses, so that's how we imitated him. Behind his back, not to his face. At a recent family reunion, we were talking about the good old days when my cousin asked me if I was the big, tough guy growing up. "Hell no," I said. "That was Vince. Even when we were kids I called him Mr. Flaminio."

Steve though, blessed with the authority of first-born status, had his with way with Vince. Vince didn't like swimming at Lake Antoine, but he liked scooping up little shells and dropping them in bread bags. What he did with them, I have no idea. I don't think he prowled the streets of Iron Mountain at night with that exoskeleton-weighted bag dispensing Charles Bronson-esque vigilante justice.

Actually, they're freshwater mollusks and have names like "warty back," "snuffbox," "monkey face" and "pistol grip." Zoologists must get a kick naming them after characters in 1930s gangster flicks— "No you listen to me, see; this is the way it's going to be, see. Wartyback and Snuffbox, you'll take out the guards, see. Monkeyface and Pistolgrip, you'll be on the lookout for coppers. I'll go behind the counter, and before I grab the loot, I'm gonna' make it with the dames, see."

Vince would wade into water no higher than the bottom of his shorts, the only person in the lake with perfectly dry swimming trunks. Although he couldn't do anything without his glasses, at least now they helped him zero in on shells on the sandy bottom. When he found one, he'd contort his body so he could grab the nugget without getting wet. He'd reach to the bottom with one arm and counter balance with the other arm, like a golfer pulling his ball out of the cup after a putt. Instead of looking down, Vince would tilt his head skyward, avoiding any chance of water contact. To be extra careful to avoid drowning, he'd hold his breath by puffing out his cheeks. It was a funny sight, Vinny the Blowfish with those thick glasses. Too bad he wasn't a Mob enforcer, he would have had a great nickname — "Yo, you better pay up or Vinny the Blowfish here is going to see to it that you sleep with his cousins." The sound of Steve thrashing through the water usually interrupted Vince's mollusk mania. Like a shark smelling blood, a hydrophobic Vince picking bivalves was too tempting for Steve to pass up. Cue the attack theme from *Jaws*.

Poor Vinny, happy as a clam picking shells, had to use every one of his muscles to fend off Steve's attack. Steve grabbed Vince and tried to dunk him. Then came cries of "Ma! Ma!" carrying over the water. One "Steve, knock it off" from Mom was enough to end the assault, and the Great White Steve slithered away, biding him time.

Steve really wasn't a bully; it's just as the oldest he commanded respect, a universal rule of birth order. It was good having an older brother to show me the ropes and correct my errors. I liked to walk around the house singing pop songs, at least as I thought they were sung. I was singing the Eagles hit, "Life is a vast plain, surely make you lose your mind ...." Lucky for me Steve heard it and said "It's 'fast lane,' dummy." That's what older brothers are for.

Kitchen Styles

Most Flaminio men, including Dad, his brother and their cousins, were called "Flip." Most of us boys in the family were Flips, too. Mom didn't grow up around Dad's family and wasn't versed in proper Flaminio nickname protocol, so we can excuse her for addressing a card to Dad on their first wedding anniversary to "Phlipp." That must be the nickname for all Phlaminios.

When we had just moved to Iron Mountain, we were hanging out a block down Maple Street. An older kid who lived down there asked us our names. When Vince told him, he said, "Like Sergeant Vince Carter on *Gomer Pyle*," the comedy about a Marine Corps barracks. The name stuck and since that day, he's been known as Carter. That's all we call him. One of my friends was there too and pleaded, "Call me Gomer." Lucky for him, no one did.

When Stephanie was a baby and she cried, it sounded like she was making a "moomin" sound, and I asked Mom, "Why is she always moomin?" She became "Moomer," and as with Carter, the name stuck. I don't think any of us in the family can ever remember calling her Stephanie. She'll always be Moomer to us. Vince and Stephanie, the two phantom Flaminios. Or is that fantom Phlaminios?

~~~

Seven boys means seven haircuts, and seven barbershop visits weren't financially feasible, so Mom assumed the duties, setting up a shop in our kitchen. She gave us buzz cuts with a pair of electric clippers. Zip, zip, zip. After a haircut, we liked to run our fingers over our heads to feel the prickly short hairs, just like a cactus. We knew enough though, not to run our hands over a cactus. Well, at least most of us did. Mom had small cactus plants around the house, and Carter showed up once with a bunch of the needles sticking in his palm. Maybe he grabbed one on a dare, or maybe he just wanted to show it who was boss. Mom had to pluck all those little prickles out of his hand with the nose foam tweezers. Those tweezers were an important weapon in our first aid arsenal.

Eventually, we grew out our hair like everyone in the 1970s. However, we still didn't have directions to the barbershop; Mom was still our kitchen-based stylist. One of her women's magazines had a hair-cutting article with step-by-step instructions. She studied hard and was a correspondence-course valedictorian. At least when she cut our hair, she didn't use a bowl. Mom didn't cut Dad's hair though. When you're the man of the house, you don't get a haircut based on the Good Housekeeping Seal of Approval, you go to a barber named Whitey Wayne.

Robert had thick, wiry, black hair, just like a Brillo pad. When his hair grew long, it didn't go straight down as most of ours did, it grew up and out. We'd joke that he looked like Conway Twitty. It didn't bother him; he'd just start singing, "Hello Darlin', nice to see ya'...."

All of us had black or brown hair, except Tony, he had fair, dirty blonde hair. Dirty as in color or dirty as in hygiene, take your pick. Once Dad's golfing buddy dropped him off and asked Dad whose kid was the blond. What's that joke about being "the mailman's kid?" Sometimes Dad called him "Thor" after the blonde Viking god of thunder or sometimes he called him "Whitey Wayne," in honor of his barber. We just had to believe Dad when he said that was his barber's name because we never saw him. Vikings and barbers were people who supposedly existed.

Sometimes, Mom's haircuts left Tony with straight-across blonde bangs. He looked like the Dutch Boy, so naturally, we felt it was our duty to point this out to him. To me, some of his haircuts looked like he was wearing a helmet, so I started calling him "Helmet Head," or affectionately, "Helmy." As he got older and my respect for him grew, I gave him a name more fitting to his growing stature — "Sir Head of Helmet."

Tears of a Clown

The year before kindergarten, Carter, Robert, and I attended Head Start, the pre-school program started by the Kennedy administration to give "disadvantaged" kids a head start on their education.

We didn't ride in a short yellow school bus as they do today. Our teachers picked us up at home in their own cars, in my case a black Chevy Impala. I guess Impalas were popular in Iron Mountain.

They served us lunch every day and I remember my first day, we had green beans. I had never eaten them before; heck I didn't even know what they were. All I knew was that I hated them at first bite. I thought I would get in trouble if I didn't eat everything on my plate, so I choked down every last one of those tax-payer funded green shoots. I think I just daydreamed about good grub, like a nice leftover bologna sandwich from Dad's lunchbox, while forcing them down,

One time at Head Start, we each lay on a piece of white butcher paper, and our teacher outlined our bodies on the paper and cut them out. We colored in our faces and clothes with crayons, and for some reason I colored my skin brown. Funny, there was a black kid in our class and he left his skin uncolored. Perhaps, the scars from the New Jersey incident were still raw, and I was looking for redemption in my own little way. The teachers taped the little kiddies to the wall, like a chain of paper dolls cut out of folded paper, and invited the moms for a showing. As they admired the twelve or so works of art, they all assumed the lone brown-skinned paperboy was the black kid in class. Nope, it was me.

We were to have a Halloween party in Head Start, so that meant costumes. That also meant I wouldn't be wearing one of those cheap, store-bought costumes — a colossal waste of money in our house. They were made of flimsy satin-like material, asbestos-free to be sure because they definitely weren't fire-retardant, and they had plastic masks held on your head with an elastic string. This was well before readily available rubber masks and before Halloween became the adult celebration it is today.

I'd be going to the party dressed as whatever Mom's creativity could conjure up with material lying around the house. She decided I would be a clown. You want to swear like a clown, you can dress like a clown. She took an oversized shirt and sewed on some red circles she cut out of cloth. I think it was more of a smock then a shirt. One-half of a chopped red rubber ball was my nose. She snipped a large rubber band and tied each end through holes she had punctured on opposite edges of the half-ball. I just slipped it over my head and ta da! Red nose. I looked like a clown in that homemade costume. But then again, that was the point.

Most of my classmates showed up as satin ghosts and monsters. I looked like a red-nosed alcoholic with a polka-dot shirt. Then I knew what they meant by the "tears of a clown." I don't know what became of my clown costume, I'm sure after Halloween it got recycled into something useful. A few years later, someone probably uttered, "Why does Moomer's diaper have red polka dots?"

~~~

One day, our class took a field trip to the soda bottling plant in Iron Mountain, where my Grandpa had worked years earlier as a delivery truck driver. Once he got in a pretty bad accident and called the plant to let them know. The first thing his boss asked was, "Are the truck and soda OK?"

Back then, soda came in glass bottles, not two-liter plastic jugs. I remember all those empty bottles coming down the line like soldiers marching in formation and then getting filled with water and flavored syrup. It must have been an important event in town because our picture was in the *Iron Mountain News*. Was the headline "Local Head Start Students Tour Soda Bottling Plant. Viet Cong Launches Tet Offensive (back page)"?

In the picture, I'm wearing a big goofy grin and a hat knitted for me by our next-door neighbor, Grandma Rahoi. It was aqua blue and had straps that buttoned beneath the chin. It looked like a World War I pilot's hat, like the Red Baron, or the Aqua Blue Baron in my case. All that was missing was a pair of goggles.

Grandma Rahoi later knitted hats for Jim and John with the same aqua blue yarn. These weren't pilot hats; they were regular knit hats with a little tassel on the top. Pilot hats were "so 1968" by then. Grandma Rahoi must have had a stash of aqua blue yarn and thought, "What am I going to do with all this yarn? I guess I'll just make some hats for the kids next door." When Jim and John were toddlers, they'd run around the house naked wearing those hats and throwing around a spongy, foam Nerf basketball. The ball was about the size of a coconut and came with a tiny backboard, hoop, and net that stuck to a wall with suction cups. You'd just toss the Nerf ball through the hoop; that's it. It sounds ridiculous now, but at the time, it was one of the best toys. To Jim and John's credit, they never tried to shove it up their noses.

"Hey, Tony Galento!"

In Iron Mountain, most blocks had an alley between two parallel streets. We shared ours with the houses on "A" Street to the south. Trash collection was along the alleys and we liked to follow the garbage men up and down, watching them toss around steel garbage cans. We were their trashy groupies.

The garbage men had big muscles, wore dirty clothes, and did gritty work. We felt right at home among them, minus the muscles. They'd empty the garbage into a bin in the back of the garbage truck; a hydraulic-powered steel blade scooped up the garbage and squeezed it into a big storage compartment. We thought that machine was the greatest invention in the world, besides maybe a revolving bucket of crispy drumsticks. Kids today don't follow garbage trucks around and marvel at the wonders of hydraulics and compaction.

Dad certainly appreciated their work too, considering all the trash generated by a household our size, and at Christmastime he'd leave them a 12-pack of beer on a garbage can. Actually, everyone in our family left one beer.

Those can tossers were characters. One of them, called "Mac," was especially good to us. My brother Robert was short and stocky, and Mac called him "Tony Galento." "Hey, Tony Galento," he'd shout to Robert in an Italian accent. We didn't know who Tony Galento was, but it made us laugh when he said it like that. After a while, he called all of us Tony Galento. It became a generic term for any Flaminio boy, just as any cola was Coke. I'm sure Mac was grateful that disposable diapers were contraband in our house— "Tony Galento, why you messa' you diaper!"

Who was this Dago that Mac joked about? "Two Ton" Tony Galento was a short, barrel-chested, Italian-American heavyweight boxer in the 1930s and 1940s. During his fighting career he had a job delivering ice. When asked why he was late for one fight, he said he had to deliver two tons of ice before the match. His appetite was legendary, and even when he was in training, he would eat several chickens and spaghetti and meatballs for dinner, chased with enough beer to fill his chest. He reportedly ate 50 hot dogs on a bet before one fight. He was famous for his "I'll moida da bum" quote about Joe Louis. On the day of his fight with Max Baer, Galento stopped at the bar he owned for his customary pasta and beer dinner. For dessert he had a pre-match warm-up, getting into a fight with his brother at the bar, who split Galento's lip. He retired from fighting in 1943 and turned to professional wrestling and acting, landing roles in *Guys and Dolls* and *On the Waterfront*.

One of the garbage men would lift rocks or pieces of asphalt shingle and pluck small, slimy slugs that lived beneath. He'd hold up one, say, "Mmm, good," and drop it in his mouth. At least that's the way it appeared to me. He'd then flex a bicep as big as a Cornish hen and say "See, they give you big muscles." We liked to sing the *Popeye, the Sailor Man* song. We were fascinated about him living in a garbage can, eating all the worms and spitting out the germs. Well, this was a garbage man with big muscles like Popeye, and those slugs are kind of like worms, so maybe he was on to something. It almost made me want to eat one of those slimy sliders.

Those garbage men liked to play tricks on us, although you

probably don't have to be Houdini when your audience is four and five-year-olds. One would "find" quarters under rocks and garbage can lids. He'd lift up a rock and say, "Look there," and there'd be a shiny quarter on the ground that he'd scoop up. Hey, where's the slug? He'd do it again, and there'd be another quarter. Knowing a good thing when I saw one, I turned up rocks left and right hoping lady luck was on my side, but every time there'd be only dirt. I figured I was just looking under the wrong rocks. He must have had a good laugh, watching me turn up rocks and come up empty-handed.

On Christmas Eve, Mac would dress as Santa and come over to entertain us. We thought he was the real McCoy. One time Dad made him a drink, and they sat on the couch having a normal conversation and enjoying their gin and tonics. I thought it was odd, Santa having an adult drink and just talking to Dad like it was any old day. But he was Santa; he could do whatever he wanted. I hoped he wouldn't drink too much because he had a lot of presents to deliver. Steve wasn't quite convinced, "You're really not Santa," he said. Steve gave his beard a tug, and Santa did a good job of covering his tracks. He let out an "Ow" and told him not to do it, because it hurt. Steve backed off, but I don't think Santa totally sold him.

Mac was a lot better Santa doppelganger than Mom. One year she bought a Santa suit for an outdoor St. Nick performance for Jim, John, Moomer and Tony. This theatre in the park required a quality, store-bought suit, not one made on her Singer sewing machine. This was no time for clowning around.

It was just like Italian comedy in the Middle Ages, *commedia dell'arte all'improviso,* outdoor theatre that relied on costumed performers and props instead of expensive scenery. Hopefully, she could live up to the standards of the one of the best medieval Italian comics, Flaminio Scala.

Mom told us older kids to use some ploy to get the four to the kitchen window on Christmas Eve, maybe we said "Look, it's the ghost of Joe the Coal Man!" She put on the Santa suit on the front porch and slung over her shoulder a bag stuffed to look like it was full of presents. I'm sure a trip to the laundry chute would have provided ample sack stuffing material. She snuck out the front door and headed to the window for her one-woman *Holiday on Ice*. Our ruse worked because there were four little noses pressed against the frosty window waiting for God knows what we told them. Santa Barbara came bounding over with that sack full of presents shouting "Ho, ho, ho" and waving to her kids. It was hard for us to keep a straight face. "Look, it's Santa," we giggle-told our pajama-clad younger siblings. Unfortunately, an oversized Santa suit on a female body isn't going to fool anyone, not even four- and five-year-old kids. Santa looked like a successful *Weight Watchers* graduate. Four voices cried in disappointed unison, "That's Mom!" After the critics' panned her, Mom canceled all future performances and just came back in through the kitchen side door. I hope she still had the receipt for that suit.

Virgin In A Bathtub

Our next-door neighbors were an older couple, Jack and Mary Rahoi. I can only imagine what they thought in 1967 when this young couple with six little kids in tow moved in next door. They were Grandpa Jack and Grandma Rahoi to us, and we couldn't have asked for better next-door neighbors. They were caring people who opened up their home to us and treated us like family.

A path in their backyard led to ours, and Grandpa Jack bordered it with flowers. That's a sign of people who get along with their neighbors. He had a big garden that took up half his backyard and butted up against our yard. Every year, he grew a nice crop of tomatoes, corn, carrots, green beans, and radishes, like a Victory Garden from the World War II years. He must have really wanted to stick it to Berlin and Tokyo. In the spring he'd spread a few truckloads of manure on his garden, and in the fall he'd have a bumper crop. Grandpa Jack and Dad were each good at fertilizing in their own ways.

Grandpa Jack took great pride in that garden, but fortunately for us that pride didn't cloud his better angels. Sometime right after we moved there, Robert came into the house saying "Apples, apples" and like a serpent showed Mom a "green apple." Mom wasn't Eve, and that was no apple.

The panic set in when Mom realized where those "apples" came from. She ran next door to Grandpa Jack's garden and saw Robert's damage. There were green tomatoes strewn all over his garden, every plant stripped bare. Apparently, the garden pest *Robertus flaminius* only targeted tomatoes. Although Mom was creative, I'm sure she realized that gluing or stapling the tomatoes back on the plants wouldn't fool anyone. With six kids next door, Grandpa Jack would have solved the caper in no time. Mom didn't want him to find the destruction before she could tell him, so she went over and spilled the beans. Luckily, he didn't get angry and just took it in stride. Maybe, he gave us a free pass because we were new neighbors. A few years later, Dad put up a metal fence (or was it a cage?) around our backyard. He installed a gate at the path to the Rahois' yard, so we could still go over for visits or veggies.

The other half of Grandpa Jack's backyard was a lawn full of clover. We liked to hunt for four-leaf clovers and have Grandpa Jack count the leaves for us. We'd run up to him in his favorite outdoor metal rocking chair and ask, "Is this one?" He'd count "One, two, three," saying his "threes" as many old Italians did in Iron Mountain, rolling the "r." "One, two, trrree." He sounded like the owl on the TV commercial when the kid asked how many licks it took to get to the Tootsie Roll center of a Tootsie Pop. We got a kick hearing him count like that. When he finished at "trrree," we'd hurry back to the lawn and pick another one. We really didn't care if we found a four-leaf clover or not, the only Irish thing we cared about was Lucky Charms cereal. We just wanted to hear Grandpa Jack count to "trrree." We also liked how he started a lot of his sentences with "By golly," but he pronounced it "gully" — "By gully, what happened to my tomatoes?"

Grandpa Jack was a retired fireman and an avid outdoorsman who kept a hunting camp north of Iron Mountain. He was a trapper and liked to show us the furry collection of beaver, otter, and muskrat pelts hanging in his garage. I wonder if any of those pelts were from vermin that had damaged the garden at his camp. Jim joked that he saw our dog Spanky's pelt hanging in Grandpa Jack's garage.

Spanky was part miniature Schnauzer, part something else, and part demon. We named him after one of the kids on *The Little Rascals* show from the 1940s. We watched it every Sunday morning before church and wanted to name our dog after one of the characters. After the infamous New Jersey Chocolate War of 1967, we didn't dare suggest Buckwheat.

I don't think Spanky ever adapted to being in a house with ten kids. He was high-strung and bit almost everyone in the family. The final straw was when he attacked Jim when he was watching TV and tore his lip up, requiring stitches. Being a typical Flaminio, Jim probably demanded Mom wait until his TV show was over before seeking medical attention. That was about it for ol' Spanky; we had to send him to the same farm we sent Shadow. If he had bitten someone outside the family, they could have sued us for everything we had. The lawyer getting one-third of that settlement would have questioned his career choice.

Grandpa Jack grew up in Channing, a small town about 30 miles north of Iron Mountain, and he had a lot of family in the area. Every Christmas Eve, the Rahois had a big family gathering, and they'd invite us for the festivities. We were the biggest contingent at the Rahoi Christmas celebration, and were just the next-door neighbors. It was a good time; there was food, fun, and adults getting liquored up and laughing. Late in the party, Santa Claus would show up with a sack full of presents for the kids. We'd all circle him and he'd reach in the sack, grab a present, and act as if he was handing it to one kid, saying, "One for ..." drawing that out and quickly turning around to shout, "you!" He'd hand the annual box of Cracker Jacks to some other kid in the now-laughing circle. He did his presentation like that every year, and we never got tired of it. One year, after another prize performance, Santa was heading out the house when Steve shouted, "Good riddance!" In his defense, he had no idea what it meant (I think). Let's see, Steve challenged our garbage man Santa and pulled his beard and told the Rahoi Santa to get lost. I guess every kid needs a mythological creature to battle. I had my werewolf and Steve had Santa.

Grandpa Jack had one of those Virgin Mary in Bathtub lawn displays, "Bathtub Madonnas," as they were known. They were popular with Italian immigrants, so naturally they were all over Iron Mountain. A statue of the Virgin Mary, arms outstretched at waist level, was placed inside a half-buried, upright bathtub. It was like a grotto, an artificial cave housing a religious icon, common in Catholic Europe. I've seen one of those outside of town with a fluorescent lime green Mary. I wonder if they make Bathtub Madonnas in New Jersey with Jacuzzis.

Grandpa Jack placed polished stones in front of his display; it was very nice. We may have picked his clover and tomatoes and run amok in his yard, but we never messed with his outdoor plumbing. Some things were off limits, even for us. There was no chance of us going to confession and saying, "Bless me Father for I have sinned. I knocked over Mary's bathtub."

Grandpa Jack told us he struck out Babe Ruth in a baseball game at the football stadium across Hughitt Street from our house. We had no reason to doubt him. He was Grandpa Jack, why would he make that up? It was common back in those days for small towns to have community baseball teams. Babe Ruth came to town on a barnstorming tour, and Grandpa Jack was on the Iron Mountain team. I don't know if Babe Ruth toured to hit home runs or for the local pitchers to strike him out, but I imagine if people paid to see the Bambino, they wanted him to swat some out of the park.

The Iron Mountain game was on October 28, 1926, in the middle of the Babe's career, so it wasn't like he was a washed up has-been. The Yankees had just lost the 1926 World Series to St. Louis and Ruth had hit forty-seven home runs for the season. He would hit sixty homers the next year and would play another nine seasons after his Iron Mountain appearance.

A photo that is part of Iron Mountain lore shows Babe Ruth with Iron Mountain pitcher Nello Tedeschi. The crowd in the photo wore typical attire for a 1920s baseball game — wool jackets, ties and hats. Granted it was October and the weather was probably a little chilly, but that's what fans wore to games even in July:

"OK, we've got our wool slacks, our wool jackets, starched white shirts and new ties. Now let's put on our fedoras and go to Wrigley Field to watch the Cubs."

"Gee, mister, it's summer and ninety degrees. Aren't you going to be hot?"

"Kid, you talk too much. Here's a nickel. Go buy yourself a cherry Coke. Oh, and tell your mother 'Thank you'."

A caption under one Ruth-Tedeschi photograph states, "Tedeschi, one of the pitchers for the opposing local team, who, together with a Channing, Michigan, pitcher succeeded in striking Ruth out." It must have been a collaborative pitching effort against Ruth. The "Channing, Michigan, pitcher" had to be Grandpa Jack. His story stands.

Babe Ruth wasn't the only world famous athlete to grace Iron Mountain stadium. According to old timers, Jesse Owens raced a horse there too. After the 1936 Olympics, Owens went on a nationwide horse racing tour, not riding them as in the Kentucky Derby, but actually running foot races, or maybe foot and hoof races, against them. At least if he broke his leg in a race, there was no chance they would "have to put him down." It's unfortunate that's what it came to for a black Olympic hero back in those days. I don't think you'd see that today, although an Olympic skater racing a horse on skates would be worth watching. Owens won some of the races; he said the trick was to run against horses that got spooked when the starter's gun went off. After Owens retired from his "second racing career," he even owned some racehorses. I guess you could say he beat them and he owned them.

When Grandma Rahoi passed away in the early 1980s, it broke Grandpa Jack's heart. He wasn't the same after that. Mom or Dad would go next door to check on him and bring him meals, and every time, poor Grandpa Jack would just start weeping over the loss of his wife. It wasn't too much longer before, sitting under a tree at his camp on a warm, sunny day, he peacefully reunited with Grandma Rahoi.

Angie Baby

Angie Godin was another one of our good, tolerant neighbors. She was a widowed, little old lady who lived in the big house across Maple Street. She had a high-pitched voice, couldn't have been more than four feet, eight inches tall, and always wore a housedress, usually a flower print. She had a mole on her face with whiskers sticking out of it. John called it a spider. Angie was the only adult we addressed by first name, and she didn't mind. She was one of those people who only needed a one-name calling card, like Madonna.

Angie rented her upstairs apartment to Awilda Kennedy, another nice, old lady. We called her Miss Kennedy; we weren't on a first-name basis with her. John couldn't say her name and called her "Waldo," so I guess it's good we were proper with her. The amazing thing about Angie and Miss Kennedy was they never confused our names. People half their age couldn't do that.

Miss Kennedy had never married. Miss Musik lived on the opposite end of Angie's block, another nice old lady who never married. It seemed like our neighborhood had a lot of transplants from Pasadena. Football teams have "book end tackles" on the offensive line; the 1200 block of West Hughitt had "book end spinsters." One night Miss Kennedy called Dad and said there was a bat darting around her apartment. He went up to her apartment, armed with a broom, and swatted it out of the park. Legend has it Dad pointed to the left corner of the living room before his at-bat. Miss Kennedy had been Dad's grade-school teacher, and I wonder if they ever imagined their paths would cross like this.

Lilac bushes in Angie's yard ran along Maple Street with an opening for the sidewalk up to her house. They were quite pleasant when they bloomed in late May. More importantly, Angie had a grape vine growing over a gazebo in her back yard. I think they were Concord grapes, the kind for making jelly. We found out quickly that when the grapes first start growing, they are hard and green, like peas. By August, they're still green, but softer and juicier. This was our favorite way to eat them, nice and tart. Why wait for them to turn purple?

When we'd go to the house next door to Angie's, we'd cut through her yard along a path we wore between her house and the gazebo. When we'd run by, it was easy to reach out and pilfer some grapes. Angie seemed to have radar when we were near because every now and then you'd hear her high-pitched voice shriek from her house, "Stay away from my grapes!" I think she was talking to us when she said that. I don't think she had a frisky boyfriend in the house getting handsy.

To Angie's credit, she never once told us to quit cutting through her yard or called our parents to unleash a wrath of grapes. I think for that reason we'd leave a few bunches on the vine, so she could enjoy some juicy purple nuggets in autumn. Considering it was her grape vine, it was probably the right thing to do.

We weren't the only kids in the family to whom Angie tolerated treat snatching. Angie's maiden name was Revolta, and she grew up in the early 1900s on the 100 block of West Hughitt. Her parents ran Revolta's Store, a small neighborhood grocery. Grandpa Flaminio and his family lived next door. Grandpa's sister Madge said when they'd go to Revolta's with a penny or so for candy, if

Angie was working, she'd let the Flaminio kids take more candy than they had money for. I bet those turn-of-the-century Flaminios were loading up on grape candy too. Ah, the circle of life. When I was in high school, Miss Musik called and asked me to come to her house to look at something very important. When a little old lady says she has something very important, you go, after exhausting every reason not to. Who knows, maybe it was a baseball card of her old boyfriend, Honus Wagner. I headed down the alley to her house, but I had to be on my toes. This could have been a trap set by a couple of cunning silver foxes. Maybe Miss Musik's story was just a decoy, and when I walked down the alley, Angie would spring out from the lilacs with a baseball bat and kneecap me — "I said stay away from my grapes, you S-O-B!"

So I showed up with healthy knees at Miss Musik's where she handed me Einstein's folly — a glass radio tube about three inches long with a hand-written note taped to it that read "Perpetual Motion?" A filament in the tube was flickering back and forth. I think it was just static electricity. Miss Musik told me I might want to take it with me when I went to college and study it. That's generosity, handing over one of the biggest scientific discoveries in history, practically gift-wrapping a Nobel Prize to some kid down the block. Looking back, that story is funny yet so innocent. I can't remember what I did with that tube. I probably gave it to my little brother John so he could gnaw on it.

We sometimes did yard work for Angie to earn some money. She had a different perspective on the worth of odd jobs than most people we worked for in the neighborhood. I think that, like a lot of people who lived through the Depression, she was frugal with money and knew what it was like when times were tough. Cutting her grass or doing some other yard chore usually earned us fifty cents, maybe a dollar. That was OK though, because Angie was good to us. Besides, we made up the difference in grapes.

Angie's stinginess inspired Carter to serenade her with his version of Helen Reddy's hit song "Angie Baby" — "Angie baby, you're a special lady, living in a world of make believe." Carter changed it to "Angie baby, you're a special lady, living in a world of nickels and dimes." He'd open the side door to Maple Street, stand on the top of the steps, sing his little ditty to Angie, then pop back in the house. He was like a cuckoo clock. The clock strikes twelve noon, the door opens, the bird cuckoos, then retreats. That was Carter with his version of "Angie Baby," only I think he did it to signal 3:27 p.m. every day.

Every now and then, when Mom went somewhere or was having twins, Angie helped out by making us lunch. She had a neat rotisserie hot dog cooker, similar to the ones at diners. When she set the cooker on the kitchen table and pushed the wieners onto the little rotisserie spikes, we sat there mesmerized, watching through a little glass window while the hot dogs rotated and cooked. Because it was food, and it was spinning, our first instinct was to go for a ride. If there were a TV show of just hot dogs cooking on a rotisserie, we would have written protest letters to the network when they canceled it.

Angie soon found someone to do her yard work even cheaper than us. Like, free. Grandpa Jack became her handy man, and she didn't have to worry about him grabbing her grapes. She called him "Sparky," and whenever Angie needed him, she'd just yell across Maple Street towards his house in her high-pitched voice, "Sparky! Sparky!" Soon Grandpa Jack would hear his master's voice and obediently cross Maple Street.

Poor Grandpa Jack, Angie put him through the wringer, but he didn't mind. When it came to physical work, he was an ox. We joked that Angie and Grandpa Jack were having an affair and would make out in her garage.

Rest in peace Angie, you were a great neighbor.

Our Big Breaks

When we were kids, we felt it was our duty to break anything of value in our house. Anything new had a 48-hour waiting period before our license to inflict damage went into effect. Our relatives in Italy were probably the last family on top of the Straight Tower in Pisa. From time to time, we'd get toys or bikes from our neighbors when their kids outgrew them. Unfortunately, we couldn't pass down toys because what kid wants broken ones. We had a no-bid contract to supply The Island of Misfit Toys on *Rudolf, the Red Nose Reindeer*.

Mom had some of those nice little Hummel statuettes on our living room shelves, bought by her mother in Germany right after World War II. They were porcelain figurines based on the drawings of Sister Maria Innocentia Hummel, and we plead guilty to breaking almost all of them. Most of the little boy and girl figurines were missing an arm or leg or even a head. I guess Mom could have just told admirers that they were from Hummel's Amputee Series. I bet some ancestral Flaminio used to own the Venus De Milo.

We bought a new couch and within the first week, some of us boys were wrestling on it when it suddenly dropped at one end. During our battle royal, one of its legs had snapped off. I can't remember what we told Dad had happened, but I'm sure none of us wanted to be the messenger. After that, we had a couch propped up at one corner with wood blocks. I think Dad used chunks of two-by-four; I know he didn't use our little kids' cubes with a letter on each side.

A few weeks later, Mom and Dad had a party at our house. It's not often they could entertain a houseful of adults. In fact, this was the only time. They were very excited and planned everything well. Of course, Mom cooked all the party food. What could go wrong?

We had to hide upstairs during the party, as this was an adults-only affair. Though frankly, it wasn't so bad that any of us felt the urge to write a diary about the experience. It was fun listening to the adult banter. Off-color jokes and laughter drifted up to us. Every now and then, one of us would sneak downstairs to the baptism room and steal some snacks.

At one point, Dad's friend Jim Walker sat on the couch. At the end with the broken leg. The couch went "ba-boomp." The blocks must have slipped, and Mr. Walker's end of the couch hit the floor. I can imagine the look on his face when the couch hit — "Did *I* do that?" I don't think this is the kind of block party Mom and Dad had in mind; their plan for the perfect party had been foiled by the wrestling match and the three-legged couch. They assured him it wasn't his fault, and Dad reset the blocks. The rest of the night, I'm sure all the partiers treated that end of the couch like it was surrounded by police caution ribbon and a tape outline of a body. After that, Mr. Walker probably went over to check out the Hummels. Careful when you pick those up.

Mr. Walker managed a men's clothing store in town, Fugere Brothers. That's where we bought our footwear, which for us was just tennis shoes or "tennies" as we called them. That was a time when you'd buy a pair of shoes from a grown man wearing a tie. Today, you buy shoes from a kid wearing a referee uniform. Are you selling me shoes or going to whistle me for traveling? We only wore Keds brand. They were black or red with three white stripes, the poor man's Adidas. Keds weren't the cheapest shoes; they were one of the nice things that Mom and Dad splurged on for us. With all those feet needing shoes, the cash register added up fast, but they saw to it that we had the Cadillac, OK maybe the Ford Granada of tennies.

We'd go in the store and not even look at the shoes; we'd just sit on a cushioned, four-legged chair and tell Mr. Walker what color we wanted. We took off a shoe and he sat on a stool right in front of us to go through that long-forgotten foot measuring ritual with the Ritz Stick, a wood ruler with shoe sizes marked on it. It had a fixed wedge on the bottom and a wedge that slid up and down the ruler to measure your size. The stick also had markings for measuring foot width. I always wondered if they made a similar device for fitting ladies with bras.

We'd rest the heel of our shoeless foot on the bottom wedge and Mr. Walker would slide the other wedge down to the top of the big toe, remove the stick, and read us the size. He'd always read it out loud, which we liked because we could hear how much our feet had grown since our last pair of shoes. After he got the shoe size, he'd walk over to the shelves and take out a box with our size. He'd sit back on the stool, pull out a tenny, unlace it for us and have us slide in the foot. Then he'd tie it nice and tight and have us get up and walk around to ensure a proper fit. Of course, it was always a perfect fit, and we'd have Mr. Walker hand us the other one, and we'd put it on ourselves. We proudly walked out of the store wearing our new shoes with the old ones in the box.

It was amazing, we were just kids, and this man in nice clothes was waiting on us hand and foot, or at least foot. It was quite an enjoyable experience. Maybe this is how foot fetishes start —"Hey lady, wanna' see my Ritz Stick?"

A Walt Disney Christmas

Like most kids, we thought Christmas was the best time of the year. I don't know how Mom and Dad did it, but every year they saved enough money to make sure we got a lot of stuff to break.

Half of the fun of the holiday season is the anticipation. We measured the time until Santa arrived by the number of episodes of the Sunday night show *The Wonderful World of Disney*. About a month before Christmas, Mom would say, "Four more Walt Disneys until Christmas!" A time-keeping method based on a television show, that's something we could relate to. I wonder why she never said, "Four more churches until Christmas?"

The TV show before Disney was *Mutual of Omaha's Wild Kingdom*, and we liked it just as much. It featured exotic wildlife in their natural setting. Actually, the wildlife scenes were "natural or created," according to the narrator at the end of the show. Usually, Marlin Perkins, the white-haired seventy-something host of the show, stood a safe distance from danger while his strapping and much younger assistant Jim was in a death-lock with some beast. I remember one episode in which a huge snake wrapped around Jim, choking him. Poor Jim was struggling for his life. The show probably then cut to a commercial with Marlin Perkins in his office, saying, "And if you find yourself in a near-death situation, a

Mutual of Omaha life insurance policy will give your family peace of mind."

About ten Walt Disneys before Christmas, the JC Penney's and Sears' Christmas catalogues arrived. They were as big as Detroit phone books, at least Motown during the muscle car era. Those glossy pages were magical to us. The Christmas editions were way better than the summer and fall catalogues. Only Mom was interested in those; we never looked at them, except maybe to check out the latest trends in ladies' undergarments. Cross-your-heart support, you don't say!

We loved paging through the catalogues, trying to figure out what we wanted for Christmas. We knew enough not to ask for the expensive gifts, for we all had a good inkling of the budgetary limits. Still, every Christmas was great, and we always received more than we expected. Thanks, Mom and Dad.

Robert always seemed to pick whatever was on the back page of the catalogue, like a tape recorder or a radio. It was usually some kind of electronic gadget. It was as if Dad would bring the catalogue home from the post office, Robert would pick it up, turn it over and slam it on the kitchen table and say, "That" without even looking. Experience taught him that whatever was on the back was usually something good. I always hoped for a back-page Easy Bake Oven to see if he'd take it.

A few weeks before Christmas, Mom made chocolate maple and chow mein candy for the family and as gifts. They're still Christmas treats for our family. She had to make batches and batches to ensure there was enough because, like a whiskey maker, she'd always lose an "angel's share." The maple candy was a little ball of chocolate with a creamy, smooth maple filling and topped with a walnut. The Oriental holiday sweets were a glob of crispy chow mien twigs smothered in chocolate — crunchy and chocolaty; they were delicious. Besides her chop suey, this was the closest we got to Chinese food. Kung Pao chocolate.

After she filled several cookie sheets with the baked sweets, she put them on the front porch to cool. This was almost a dare, putting them out there because the front porch door was in the living room. Although the candy was under constant surveillance, Mom couldn't watch it forever, and we always snuck some. I'm sure she expected that.

~~~

After what seemed an eternity of waiting, Christmas morning finally arrived. We couldn't wait to see what Santa brought us. Maybe he brought along his helper, *Dominic the Italian Christmas Donkey,* Italian-American novelty singer Lou Monte's yuletide jackass. We woke around four o'clock in the morning and congregated at the top of the stairs, looking like a rugby scrum; one little push would have sent us tumbling down like dominoes. We were right next to the UFO viewing port, but I felt safe with a nine-person buffer between that window and me. Anyway, would flying saucers really be out causing trouble on the morning we celebrate the birth of the Savior?

We couldn't go downstairs until Mom and Dad were good and ready and awake, and that wasn't four in the morning. After prodding, one of us succumbed to peer pressure and snuck downstairs to peek at the presents under the tree. Actually, with ten kids, presents were under the tree, and around the tree, and on chairs and couches. According to local legend, if you looked at the presents before everyone was there to open them, they would "disappear." Tempting fate, we always went one at a time to take a look-see. The visually challenged among us were probably the safest. Even if their eyes were directly pointing at the presents, they weren't really looking at them. The first one down came back and excitedly relayed the good news. Then someone else would go down and confirm the story. This was repeated until there were multiple witness statements. No presents ever vaporized either.

Eventually, one brave soul went to the "Laugh-In" window to Mom and Dad's room to ask if we could come down. It was like a confessional screen; you'd whisper to it, but couldn't see anyone behind it; however, you knew salvation was dispensed from the other side. But instead of an "Our Father" prayer penance, we got a, "Get upstairs." Mom and Dad were both too tired to pop their heads out of the shutters. The bearer of bad news trudged upstairs with a dejected look; we all could read the body language. It wasn't until around six in the morning when we finally had worn Mom and Dad down that twenty bare feet thundered down the stairs. It was a shoe salesman Jim Walker bolt up in the middle of the night, drenched in sweat, Ritz-stick nightmare.

One Christmas I chose a pair of wooden skis from the JC Penney catalogue. All the skiers at the local resort, Pine Mountain, had nice fiberglass Rossignol skis. Even though our family economics kept me from skiing at Pine Mountain, I didn't care because I had my nice, wooden Jean Claude Penneys. By this time, I had real boots and didn't have to ski wearing bread bags. Not real ski boots, just real winter boots.

Bread bags were still winter survival gear in Iron Mountain for a little while after our sled ride. In the early '70s, almost all the school kids wore those black, shin-high, rubber galoshes with the buckles, with bread bags over their shoes to keep them dry and help squeeze them into the boots. All the kids in town wore the same boots as bankers.

After those black beauties went out of style, we went through our "swamper" phase. Those were rubber, military-green, laced boots popular in the Louisiana bayou. They kept our feet dry and didn't require bread bags but weren't well insulated. I guess that doesn't matter if you're the Roubicheaux kids in the bayou, but for the Flaminios in the Upper Midwest, it's a concern. At one point, practicality and thermal considerations led us to snowmobile boots. These were rubber boots with nylon from the ankle to the shin and insulated inserts to keep our feet warm. We could buy them at most stores in town right off the shelf, no pampered Ritz-stick measuring needed.

The best thing about my wooden skis was that they were aqua

blue, just like my long-gone knit pilot hat. I could imagine the man at the wooden ski factory with a can of aqua blue paint and a brush lovingly painting my skis. If only I still had that hat, I would have looked so good. As I understood it, coordinated fashion on the slopes was almost as important as skiing ability.

Since a season pass at Pine Mountain was out of the question, Mom had a great idea for a backyard hill. She told us to gather Christmas trees, pile them up, and then cover them with snow. So Robert, Carter, and I went around taking neighbors' Christmas trees. Not from their living rooms, but when they put them out for pick-up by the city disposal crews. When we had piled and covered them, we had a giant ski hill about five feet tall at its peak. Perfect umbrella jumping height. It wasn't Pine Mountain, but it was a pine mountain.

We went down it a few times, taking turns on my skis, and to our dismay, came to a dead stop at the base of the "hill." We tried sledding a few times, but that wasn't much better. The thrill of victory wore off quickly, and now we were stuck with all those Christmas trees. We dug them out and followed the "trail of tears" sledding path from a few years earlier and dumped them in the woods by the City Park.

Behind the park, there were three ski jumps right next to each other : Mini-Mite, Mighty-Mite and Miron. The largest ski jump in the area is at the Pine Mountain resort, it's used for international competitions. Mini-Mite was just a snow-covered hill with a little jump at the end. Mighty-Mite was a wooden ski jump painted orange. Last was Miron, also wooden and the biggest of the three. The City Park jumps were for the youth ski-jumping program, which hoped to produce world-class ski jumpers. However, I wouldn't say this was a "way out of the ghettos" for kids from Iron Mountain.

After the backyard slope agony of defeat, Carter pined for a bigger challenge and took my blue boards and went with John and Tony Sacchetti to the ski jumps behind the park. The Sacchettis lived down the alley from us. Their dad's name was Joe, and when he and my Dad were kids, they caddied together at the golf course at the end of Hughitt Street, the Pine Grove Country Club. The caddies called him Joe-Pete because his name was Joseph Peter Sacchetti. He had slicked back black hair and a moustache; he always had a cigar in his mouth. He looked like a Mob boss, but then again a lot of guys in Iron Mountain looked like a *capo*. Before he smoked his cigars, he'd always lick them first to get them nice and wet. I never knew why he did that. I was surprised he could light those things with so much spit on them.

Carter said he and John Sacchetti actually went off the Miron jump. I wasn't sure he was telling the truth, but I wanted to believe he did it on my blue skis. That ski jump is intimidating. Maybe, he meant the orange Mighty Mite jump.

As I was admiring him for his ski jumping prowess, he figured it was a good time to say, "Oh and your skis broke."

Good timing on his part. I really wasn't mad because I thought of our cheesy little backyard hill and then Carter jumping off a real ski jump with his ski goggles/Coke bottles and my skis shattering on impact. I was impressed by his courage. At least he was upholding our canon law of breaking things.

Jed Clampett — DANGER RADIATION

Our first TV in Iron Mountain was an ancient nineteen-inch black and white model that rode with us from New Jersey. It had a hand-turn channel dial, "clack, clack, clack." I think the model was a prop in the Raquel Welch movie *1,000,000 B.C.* We only got about six stations, this was before cable television, so it's not like we'd get carpal tunnel syndrome from channel surfing.

In the early '70s, we replaced it with a color television from Sears, one of those big rest-on-the-floor sets that could double as a book or cereal box shelf. Ah, Ginger and Mary Ann in color. Mrs. Howell, whatever. The new set had a manual channel dial, but it was color so we didn't care if we wrist-twisted all night. Finally, we saw the NBC peacock in its natural or created habitat. We loved that new television and offered it zombie-like submission for years. We were Manchurian candidates and the TV was dealing cards. I remember how excited we all were the first night in living color. Before going to bed, I sprawled my torso across the top of the TV and laid my head down, my chest cavity absorbing the warmth radiating from the cathode ray tube. I was embracing the new addition to our family; one that wasn't Dr. Klingler's fault.

When we watched a show, we'd park ourselves right in front the

TV, no more than three feet from the screen. We would either sit with our legs crossed, Indian style, or lie on our stomachs with our hands propping up our faces. Perfect positions, the screen at eye level. We usually had our mouths open too. We looked like the Vienna Boys Choir watching television.

After we got the color television, Marie became a radiation buff. She was sure that that color TVs emitted radiation, and if you sat too close, radiation stops your growth. If you were small, it was probably because of radiation. I don't know what piqued Marie's curiosity about this. Of course, Marie was right in the front row watching T.V. with the rest of us. As our dentist can attest, instead of dental decay, we focused on nuclear decay.

After taking communion at church one Sunday, we sat in the pew watching others return from eating Jesus when a real tiny girl walked by. When we got home, Marie said, "Did you see that little girl at church. I bet she had radiation." Whatever you say, Madame Curie. Little did Marie know that in a few years the microwave oven revolution would hit America and eventually Hughitt Street. Then she'd have to worry about the Hiroshima of household appliances.

Dad watched TV from the couch against the wall on the opposite side of the room. With a bunch of kids sitting inches from the television, Dad had an obstructed view seat, and more often than not, a head blocked his view. If it was me, Dad would say, "Tom, head work," and the offending melon was promptly moved from his sight line.

The only time Dad got as close as we did to the TV was in 1968. Early one morning, we were at the kitchen table reading. Dad was asleep upstairs after finishing the night shift. Mom turned on the news, and the big story was Robert Kennedy's assassination the night before. Panicked, Mom raced to the bottom of the stairs and yelled, "Flip, Flip, Kennedy died!" Robert was at the table and parroted Mom, "Flip, Flip, Kennedy died." That's one of my most vivid, early memories in Iron Mountain. Dad bolted down the stairs in his boxer shorts and knelt on the carpet right in front of the TV, settling in one of the six little kid remnants. Like the rest of America, he was trying to make sense of the killing of another Kennedy.

~~~

Watching TV in the summer on hot, humid, air conditioner-free nights was a sweaty affair with twelve bodies in the living room. I guess you could say we were in our sweat lodge on a vision quest. We had a floor fan to cool us off, and we'd set it on high to make sure it really moved that thick, hot, stale air. We'd configure ourselves on the floor to make sure we all got our fair share of that muggy breeze. The fan would whip up quite a gust, but not so much that it knocked the couch off its blocks. Because it was summer, we had to watch re-runs of our favorite shows, usually a 1970s cop drama— *Barnaby Jones*? Wait, that's Jed from *The Beverly Hillbillies*, what's he doing in a jacket and tie? Maybe we'd watch *Police Story* with *Monday Night Football* wise guy Don Meredith in his recurring role.

Our favorite cop show was *Hawaii Five-O*. The opening to that show was the best in television history with that huge wave on Waikiki Beach and the mesmerizing theme song. We always got a good laugh during the character introduction: "Jack Lord as Steve McGarret," "James MacArthur as Danno," and then they'd get to our favorite "Kam Fong as Chin Ho." Why even bother changing his name?

One of Steve's favorites and mine was *Monty Python's Flying Circus*, the English sketch comedy shown later at night on the PBS station. That British humor struck a chord with us, maybe it was because we were born in England and felt a kinship with those guys. Our interest in the show paid off handsomely one night. They showed a skit where a man walked into a little corner store, and the lady behind the counter was topless. I don't think she said anything; she just stood there with a huge grin and those big breasts staring us in the face. This was before "HBO" and "Showtime", so we never saw nudity on TV. Thank you educational television for filling the void. We turned and looked at each other with open mouths, but then again that's our everyday TV face. If that's how store clerks dress for work in England, why did we ever leave?

Monty Python had one skit about Spam, the pressed meat product in a can. It was set in a restaurant, where the Brits were singing the praises of Spam, everyone was ordering Spam. I loved that skit, and I liked walking around the house shouting "Spam" in a Cockney accent, not the proper English accent of the show. When Mom asked what we wanted for dinner, I'd say, "Spam!" Or I'd just open the refrigerator, look inside and say, "Got any Spam? I like Spam!" in my working class British.

One night, Dad surprised me and gave me a can of Spam. I think he was calling my bluff. The tin packaging was so appealing — nice colors, compact and functional. After he gave it to me, I caressed the little tin can, admiring it and feeling it's weight, like someone holding a Rolex for the first time. I couldn't believe I had a can of Spam. I twisted the little key opener around the top of the can and popped off the lid. After that, instinct took over and I just flipped it over and slammed the Spam on the table to force the meat out. Wow, it's the exact same shape as the can. Well it was out, so I tried it. So, um, anyway, Spam is popular in Hawaii. It was introduced to the Pacific Islands during World War II when it was a staple for American fighting men. Did Kam Fong/Chin Ho have a clause in his contract requiring a can of Spam every day for lunch while taping *Five-O*?

Carter had his signature phrase, too. He liked to belt out the line "I couldn't sleep at all last night," emphasizing and drawing out the "all," from "Tossin' and Turnin'" by Bobby Lewis. The TV comedy *Happy Days* played the line for scene change music. Carter adopted it as an exclamation point after an innocuous victory. Get the high score on some game— "I couldn't sleep at all last night!" Get the last bowl of cereal— "I couldn't sleep at all last night!" Throw you to the floor and pin you— "I couldn't sleep...." How many times on their wedding night did his wife Anne have to hear that?

In 1973, Elvis Presley's Hawaii concert was beamed into America's living rooms. We knew of Elvis but couldn't care one way or another about him. Isn't Hawaii for Don Ho? Or Chin Ho? Mom was a different story, and that night the TV was hers. We got a kick out of seeing her right in front of the tube like us, only she was kneeling down, showing proper respect to the King. When Elvis would sing and gyrate, Mom would slap her hands on her knees and sway her head and body side-to-side with the music. We thought it was so funny watching Mom being a teenager again. For this one moment, she wasn't Barb Flaminio, mother of ten kids coming at her from every direction wanting something. She was Bobbi Hazus, class valedictorian who had just dumped her salutatorian boyfriend for the prom king of rock and roll.

~~~

In the winter, everyone wanted a heated seat for watching TV. The toasty air from the furnace blew through registers — heaters we called them— at the bottom of the walls throughout the house. The heater on the living room wall opposite the television was the prime TV viewing location on cold winter nights, and it was worth fighting for. It wouldn't have been too farfetched to camp in front of it at five o'clock in the morning, waiting for a seven p.m. show, like someone waiting outside a store for the next version of Microsoft Windows "that probably will never be available again."

I liked sitting in front of it, Indian style with both my hands behind my back. The warm air washing over me felt so good during Saturday night episodes of *The Carol Burnet Show*, one of our favorites. As usual, there was a funny skit with Harvey Korman, undoubtedly cracking up, and with luck, Tim Conway was on too. Once Carol Burnet started singing "I'm so glad we had this time together" to end her show, I knew it was bedtime. It was almost as if I was singing to the heater through her.

We all liked to lie on the floor in front of the heater, snuggled under a blanket. If we could have, we would have spent the whole night there. Unfortunately, our dog Spanky was stiff competition for that delicious warm air, and he didn't care what show was on. When he lay in front of it, all bets were off. He'd even displace us from the spot with a few growls. We were no match for him; he retired to that farm the undisputed heavyweight champion. The consolation prize was the heater on the opposite side of the wall, but it was in the kitchen. All that got us was a heated ringside seat for the next baptism.

Besides watching TV, my other favorite pastime in front of the heater was reading *MAD Magazine*. Robert liked it too. All we needed was a stack of those magazines and we were in our own little world. (A stack of a different kind of magazine held my attention, too, but not in front of the heater.) I kind of looked like the *MAD* cover boy, Alfred E. Neuman, and lest I forgot, Mom would remind me. Take a look at my kindergarten picture, with those big, floppy ears sticking out and that "What, Me Worry?" grin and you'll see what I mean. Finally, I have a twin too. Those big ears were the reason I later grew out my hair, to cover them and spare the public. I always said I was born with fully developed ears and it took years for my head to grow in proportion.

I would be reading a *MAD* magazine in front of the heater, and I'd be laughing hysterically and John would come over and ask, "What's so funny? Show me what's so funny?" I'd ignore him and then he'd start to beg. Of course, I wouldn't tell him. It was one of those, "You had to be there's." Robert and I both loved the exploits of Roger Kaputnik, a recurring character in "The Lighter Side" cartoon panel. He was the middle-aged neighborhood boor with black horn-rimmed glasses, the one who everyone wanted to avoid. We didn't have any neighbors like that— neighbors we just wanted to avoid. I'm sure, at least I hope, our neighbors would say the same thing.

Sooner or later when we were all flopped on the floor watching

TV, we'd start dozing off. That was Dad's cue for the bugle call to send the troops to lights out. His favorite sayings were "Good night, nurse" or "Hit the road," and when he said it, we marched right upstairs, no questions asked. There was no whiney "No, I don't want to go to bed" in our house. And not once did I get up off the floor and tell someone to "move their f****'n head."

Who Are You Wearing?

We weren't fashion savvy kids, but then again we did grow up in the 70s. Our wardrobe was an assortment of brightly colored, striped, plaid, checked and hounds-tooth double-knit and polyester pants and shirts that didn't match. We looked like we were on shore leave from the Yellow Submarine. Today, you call polyester "micro-fiber" to remove the shame. There was a clothing line called Garanamals with shirts and pants tagged with animals that you matched to ensure the clothing was coordinated. If we'd worn Garanamals, we would have matched donkeys with catfish.

Blue jeans weren't daily attire for us until the mid 1970s. Usually, they weren't Levis, more likely J.C. Penney Plain Pockets or Sears Toughskins, the less expensive brands. You had to pay a premium for that little red tag on the back pocket. We even had jeans a notch below the Sears and Penney's brands, Big Yanks, a long-forgotten brand Mom bought at ShopKo, our regional department store. I don't think they sold Big Yanks in Alabama. They looked like the dungarees that Navy sailors wear. Of course, like everyone, we only wore bell-bottom jeans. We called straight-legged pants "stove pipes," and no one would dare wear them, at least until it was deemed socially acceptable in Iron Mountain, around 1980, I think.

I had a short-sleeved sweatshirt with Archie Bunker's face on it, and "Archie Bunker for President" printed around the picture. Now that's style. It must have been my good short-sleeved sweatshirt because I wore it to church. You couldn't wear a Gumby shirt to Sunday Mass, that's inappropriate.

Mom supplemented our off-the-rack fashions with rummage sale *haute couture*. With ten kids, second-hand clothing was a cost-effective wardrobe expansion strategy. We'd joke she bought our used clothes at "Barb's Boutique." Heck, we might have had third-hand clothes, too. Our clothes had so many hands, they were probably worn by a six-armed Hindu goddess.

Clothing from the used-garment district cost a dime or a quarter, so we could shop with money found under a couch cushion. The only concern was wearing your friends' old clothing. When I was in grade school, one of my friends showed me how the clasp on the front zipper on my shirt could hold a pen.

"How'd you know that?" I asked.

"Because that used to be my shirt," he said. Ouch.

When Mom returned with her rummage bounty, she'd sit on the couch and hold up the shirts one at a time to start the bidding. Hey, is that a Jimmy Walker t-shirt that says "DYN-O-MITE!"? Dibs on that! A new Sunday shirt for church. If she bought something we'd roll our eyes at, like a rhinestone-studded shirt, she'd say, "You can wear it for just knockin' around." Anyone with the fashion sense to wear an Archie Bunker sweatshirt isn't going to wear just anything for "knockin' around."

Mom also told us we could start a new fashion trend with her rummage sale duds. You watch, soon all the kids will be wearing long-sleeved, ruffled, peach-colored shirts from prom tuxedos.

Of course, we were devoted to the hand-me-down philosophy. And hand-me-up and hand-me-sideways. The first four and last three boys were close in age and size, so we could really multi-task with our clothes. When Carter caught us wearing a hand-me-down, he'd let us know it.

He'd clap his hands and sing "Hand me down, hand me down, hand me down my silver trumpet, Gabriel." That was a song from grade-school music class, and it was the most spiritual prose we'd hear at home. That and Dad's frequent use of "goddammit."

~~~

When Steve was in kindergarten, he had a pair of red leather ankle boots with rounded toes. They had gold metal rings on the sides too; decorative bling that could be used to yank up the boots. I was jealous. They kind of reminded me of pirate boots, like the ones worn by the cartoon pirate cat, Puss 'n' Boots. I don't know where Mom got those beauties. You couldn't buy boots that cool and that funky at any store in Iron Mountain. Maybe she got them from a neighbor, or maybe she bought them at a rummage sale. Maybe she strong-armed the Sly and Family Stone tour bus.

I liked to walk with Mom to see Steve and Marie off to kindergarten, and I watched with envy as they boarded their bus. I couldn't wait until next year when I'd get to ride in that crowded, yellow kiddie barge, and not have to go to Head Start in a black Impala with a student-head count in the single digits. With any luck, I'd be high-stepping on the bus wearing those crimson gypsy loafers.

One day, Steve came home from school excited about the exercises he had learned in gym class. He cleared the living room floor and demonstrated for us, putting his hands on his hips and alternately kicking his legs straight out. Right, left. Right, left, like a caffeinated Cossack at a May Day parade. Alas, those boots danced their last rumba and didn't have a spin in the hand-me-down cycle. Only Steve was blessed to have worn them. Sly must have tracked them down.

Some Home Cookin'

We didn't have the nicest clothes or best bikes, but I'd take Mom's home cooking over a new pair of Levis or a shiny Schwinn any day. With ten kids and a tight budget, we never went out for hamburgers or pizza. But we didn't care because we ate so well at home, except maybe for pizza; there were great pizza joints in town. Food was our biggest expense and sometimes we really had to stretch the wallet to cover the groceries, but we never missed a good meal. Sure we lived hand-to-mouth, but I don't care what that old guy's dietary recommendation was in the Grape Nuts cereal commercial ("I'm Euell Gibbons. Ever eat a pine tree? Many parts are edible), we never had to choose between having a Christmas tree or eating it.

Every Monday, supper (we never called it dinner) was pasta. No special reason, it just happened that way. Italian families declare their favorite pasta and ours was spaghetti, rigatoni, and a macaroni we shamefully called "springs" because that's what it looked like. I found out years later it's rotini. I guess it wouldn't seem right for a working class family of twelve to eat angel hair pasta or linguini with clam sauce. With apologies to San Lorenzo, the patron saint of pasta, we never had olive oil either. San Lorenzo was a martyr who was grilled alive, and religious paintings show him surrounded by flames holding a grill.

We almost always had a red meat sauce with our spaghetti, meatballs occasionally. Some Italians on the north side of Iron Mountain called their red sauce "gravy," but gravy was what we put on our Sunday mashed potatoes. Mom always made her sauce in a big, silver-colored cast-iron pot. The pot was only for a small lineup of culinary masterpieces, and spaghetti was first string. If I saw it today, I'd immediately think of the house on Hughitt Street and a nice, hot plate of spaghetti.

After Mom cooked and drained the spaghetti, she'd place it in big bowl, throw in a few cups of the sauce, and stir it in, the steamy macaroni absorbing that tomatoey goodness. She'd give us each a serving, and we'd all use the cup to scoop extra sauce from the silver pot. At the end of the meal, she combined the remaining spaghetti with the sauce in the pot, a perfect leftover.

Anyone who likes spaghetti knows it's just as good the next day out of the refrigerator. I don't know what kind of magic happens in that frigid air overnight, but the next day it's transformed into a dish best served cold. Sometimes, I'd just open the refrigerator and eat the cool pasta right out of the pot. With a fork, not my hands. With ten kids, the refrigerator door was always open, mostly because we were scanning the menu. That was a sore point with Dad; he complained that someone could read a book by our refrigerator light.

Once Mom made fettuccine from scratch. They're long, flat noodles and the name means "little ribbons" in Italian. For someone of eastern European descent, she did pretty well with egg, flour, and elbow grease. After she made the noodles, she hung them to dry in the kitchen on the wood dowels of a clothes-drying rack she lugged up from the basement. I'm sure she removed the socks and underwear beforehand. Making homemade pasta is a lot of work. After we devoured it in no time, as usual, Mom conceded to the Creamette pasta company and the rack permanently returned to its rightful place.

Mom also took one stab at chicken cacciatore (in Roman-speak, chicken hunter style). This is chicken braised in tomato sauce and served with pasta. I don't know what inspired Mom to cook this. Maybe she read about it on the back of a rigatoni box. I thought she was calling it "kitchen cacciatore." I guess I couldn't make the connection that it was a chicken dish, so the word "chicken" should probably be in the name. I don't think she ever tried cooking fork tenderloin; I heard it's a pig meat.

No one liked it — her only dish we shunned. We liked chicken, and we liked tomato sauce, but these two great tastes did not taste great together. Mom could have put the chicken in one bowl, the tomato sauce in another and we would have been *i bambini felici*. Together, it was a vinegar and baking soda volcano.

Friday was always hamburger night, and I can still hear Mom slapping the burgers into patties and the meat sizzling in the pan. The only bad thing about hamburger Friday was the fried burger aroma permeating the house and burrowing into our clothes. Every Friday night, we smelled like short-order cooks. It reminded me of the spray deodorizer commercial where two "proper" women walk into a friend's house and comment on the "nest odor." They were wearing nice, conservative church dresses and white gloves with their purses draped over their forearms; they looked like refugees from the set of *Ozzie and Harriet*. The commercial went like something like this:

Judgmental woman #1: "Fried fish last night, dear?"

Judgmental woman #2: "I thought George gave up cigars?"

That commercial hit too close to home. It could have been our house they had walked into. I couldn't understand why their younger and better-looking friend would have them over. I wished she'd just throw those old bags out.

We stored our bulk meat inventory in a large chest freezer in the basement, right next to the clothes dryer. You never know when you'll need frozen burger while you're folding clean underwear. The freezer was about the size of a casket, and it stored cold dead meat. Very appropriate. We stored loaves of bread in there too, but we devoured sandwiches so fast we probably never thawed the bread. Nothing like eating a bologna sandwich and getting an ice cream headache. In the summer, Mom thawed the frozen meat on the Travelall's sun-baked black roof. We didn't need a microwave oven with defrost; ultraviolet radiation from the sun god was good enough.

One Friday, she had put a couple of pounds of frozen burger on the mobile defroster when she realized she had to run to Peoples' Supermarket, a neighborhood grocery store. She drove to the store and back with the iced protein on the roof. I'm sure she knew it was there and was well aware that a frozen object will thaw quicker if hot air is flowing over it. If Mom was an expert on anything, it was thermodynamics. It seemed that every other week she was telling us, "The rate at which heat is conducted through a body per unit cross-sectional area is negatively proportional to the temperature gradient existing in the body." Who were we to argue with Mom?

I thought Peoples' Supermarket sounded like a Marxist collective in North Korea. I'm sure Peoples' sold red cabbage. I wonder if they sold kim chee too. I know for a fact they sold porketta (properly "porchetta" in the motherland), an Iron Mountain Italian classic— salted, boneless pork roast stuffed with garlic, rosemary and fennel. In our town, everyone put that spicy hog on crusty Italian rolls. Our favorite porketta was from Peoples. It must have been the personal touch of the owner, Mr. Cerasoli.

Mom did the bulk grocery shopping at another Soviet-friendly store, the Red Owl, a now-defunct supermarket chain. The Red Owl logo was a big red owl head, angry looking, as if it were saying "Who *you* looking at?!" The Red Owl head at the Iron Mountain store was elevated on some posts on the roof. I think barn swallows nested under that too. The store was across from the Kentucky Fried Chicken, so with every bucket revolution Colonel Sanders and Comrade General Owl had a stare down. So Mom is Lithuanian and Ukrainian; her dad looked like Joseph Stalin, and she shopped at the Red Owl and Peoples' Supermarket. No wonder she supported America's healthcare overhaul.

When Mom shopped at Red Owl, she needed at least two shopping carts, mostly for cereal. After she paid the cashier, she'd get S&H Green Stamps, based on how much money she spent. Those Sperry and Hutchinson Company trading stamps looked like little green postage stamps with the S&H logo. You'd lick the gummy glue on the back, stick them in a booklet and redeem full booklets for housewares, such as toasters, coffee pots and wooden spoons. Mom had her green stamps and Dad had his postage stamps. As they say, married couples need separate interests to maintain their own identities.

Saturday was chili night, and Mom cooked it in the big, silver cast iron pot. That pot was our seasoned wok — don't clean it, just wipe it off to keep the flavor in the steel. The chili lasted through Sunday, and after we emptied the pot, Mom prepped it for spaghetti's turn from the on-deck circle.

Sunday lunch was always at one o'clock in the afternoon, and it was our favorite non-Monday meal; exclusively meat and potatoes. My favorite was roast beef because Mom usually made Yorkshire pudding with it, a traditional Sunday side dish in England. It's nothing like dessert pudding. It's a quick bread which is baked in a pan, and it's made with flour, egg, milk and, most deliciously, the beef pan drippings. When done, it's golden-brown, crisp and puffy. The bread "puffs" usually deflate after it's pulled from the oven. If they were stubborn, we liked to pop them with a fork.

After one typically good Sunday meal, Carter came to a different gastronomic conclusion than the other eleven satisfied customers. Carter the New Yorkshire Times food critic didn't mince words with his blunt review: "That was a good meal, Mom. Thanks. Lumpy potatoes and burnt meat." Huh?! Typical critic, he had an opinion out of step with everyone else. I don't know how many stars Carter gave Mom's dish, but the most amazing thing was that he wasn't seeing them after that review.

Mom also made great chop suey and Spanish rice. Chop suey is an American pork and rice dish. You can tell by the name that it's not authentic Chinese. Her secret ingredient for Spanish rice was mustard, surely common in the kitchens of Madrid. Another of Mom's savory classics was a meat pastry. She'd lay out a long piece of bread dough, pile on cooked, seasoned, ground beef and then roll and fold the dough. It was a meat Yule log. After it was baked, she'd crosscut sections so we each got a nice stump and then we'd bathe it in tomato sauce. We loved it. She had an ingenious name for this dish, "meat rolled up on a bun." Simple and to the point. There might be a correct name for it, but hers sums it up nicely.

In the summer we always had bulk-size wide-mouth jars of hamburger-sliced dill pickles, our traditional seasonal food, like watermelon for Texans. Those pickle slices were so tangy, my mouth still waters just thinking about them. Then again, our mouths watered thinking of cucumber seeds, knowing they'd sprout into cucumbers that would eventually find their way into a pickle jar. Wide-mouth to us meant wide enough for our hands, and after playing outside, we'd plunge our grimy, sweaty hands into the jar like a cat pawing at goldfish. After a few rounds of bobbing for pickles, that murky juice wouldn't let any wavelength of light pass through. We didn't worry though; we knew that vinegar and salt kills germs. There was never a case of salmonella or botulism in our family, at least that we were aware of.

~~~

Mom's excellent cooking skills didn't necessarily transfer to her kids. Steve was pretty smart; and you'd think making a cheeseburger would be in his skill set. He slapped the patty into shape as he'd seen Mom do countless times. He put it on the hot pan and when it sizzled, he was in business. After he flipped it, he took an American cheese single out of its wrapper and laid it on top. He must have really wanted the cheese to melt fast because then he flipped the burger cheese-side down. Yum, the acrid smell of burnt cheese product. Good thing Steve became an accountant, and cooking with cheese wasn't his craft.

Marie liked to bake cakes and cookies, and in an episode of sibling rivalry, Kathy baked a, um, "cake." If she had tried to fry a cheeseburger to one up Steve, it would have been more of a sizzling rivalry. Kathy laid out the ingredients and went to work. The batter looked fine, so she poured it in the pan and placed it in the preheated oven. After she pulled the cake out of oven, she put it on the front porch to ice it. Not for the chocolaty icing, the front porch doubled as our walk-in cooler.

When the cake came in from the cold, something wasn't right. It was dry and crumbly; it looked like a big, crushed cookie. If her baking rivalry with Marie were a football game, Kathy had the ball, and it was fourth and long. It was a "punt" cake. After a little spy work, we discovered that instead of flour for the batter, Kathy had used instant milk powder. Uh oh, she'd broken into half of Mom's half-and-half stash. Flour comes in a bag labeled "Flour," but she used an ingredient that comes in a big box labeled "Instant Milk" that has a picture of a glass of milk on it. To Kathy it must have meant "the flour in this box can be used to bake a cake that tastes good with milk, like the glassful shown on this box." Maybe it's a good thing she never finished it, there's no telling what she would have used for icing. We might have heard Mom say, "What happened to all my Dippity-Do?"

Moomer always made a Chex Mix treat. She found the recipe on the back of a Chex cereal box. Finally, years of reading the back of those boxes paid off. She always made the mix in an old, beat-up yellow pot. Apparently, the silver bullet was off limits. After she heated the pot, she'd drop in a glob of butter. It was margarine actually; we never had butter. We usually had Blue Bonnet margarine; the packaging had a picture of a lady wearing a blue bonnet (of course). She was my pilot hat soul mate. Mom and Dad always called the margarine "oleo"; that must have been a 1950s thing. After the margarine melted, she'd throw in Corn

Chex, pretzels, some nuts and loads of garlic salt. It stunk up the whole kitchen, and she was the only one who ate it. I was surprised one of us didn't try making that dish with Count Chocula. My favorite condiment, or maybe favorite food, was mustard. Plochmans was the best, but I didn't discriminate. No matter what brand Mom bought, it would morph into a yellow stain on my clothes, even on my socks. My brother Jim joked that he could throw my clothes in boiling water to make a soup to feed the poor. The condiment blotches on my clothes are a bellwether for America's changing palate. Today, you're likely to find my shirts spattered with dried hot sauce.

Before squeeze bottles, mustard came in glass jars and I'd just spoon it out and eat it. No spoon, no problem— an index finger dipped in the jar holds about as much. Hey, fingers in the pickle jar didn't harm us. Shortly after Neil Armstrong's lunar landing, the mustard moguls figured out a way to dispense their product efficiently: the squeeze bottle. The last few drops in a glass jar were easy to get at, just fish it out with a butter knife or a finger (but not a Butterfinger). The squeeze bottle put up more of a fight for its dregs. When it sputtered on empty, that was my Siren call to cut it in half with a steak knife to expose the residual nectar.

When we were older and came home late at night, we liked to raid the refrigerator. We didn't need Mom's permission anymore for fractions of a snack. One night, I made a sandwich, and the mustard jar was on its last legs, so I took a butter knife and started working the jar trying to get the last few dollops of golden goodness. Clank, clank, clank the knife went against the glass; the sound rang through the darkened house. For whom the bell tolls? It tolls for the mustard freak. Everyone was asleep, maybe not anymore. I finally got my anorexic-sized portion of mustard and dripped it on my sandwich. The next morning Carter thanked me for interrupting his sleep. The saddest sound in the world to me wasn't the slurping sound at the end of a Nestlé's Quick chocolate milk; it was the clanging of a vacated mustard jar.

~~~

Dad didn't cook, but back in those days, most men didn't. The man brought home the bacon, and the wife fried it. That's the way it was. He worked two jobs to put food on the table, and his only obligation was uncooked food. The only time I remember Dad cooking was when Mom and Tony went to visit her family in Pennsylvania.

With no one else to cook, Dad had to throw a life vest to his inner Julia Child —that lone estrogen castaway drowning in his sea of testosterone. In the early 1970s, guys weren't into cooking like they are today. There was no Food Network with male celebrity chefs, there was only the *Galloping Gourmet*, a cooking show with a British guy who'd make some high-falutin' dinner and then drag an audience member on stage to share it with him. The fact it was an English bloke on the cooking show says a lot about American men's cooking skills back then. This was the era of the Marlboro Man, and when the commercial said, "Come to where the flavor is. Come to Marlboro country," the narrator wasn't referring to the spice section in the grocery store.

Dad would tell us stories about his daily lunch in basic training, chipped beef on toast. They called it "sh*t on a shingle." We hoped that wouldn't be his inspiration for his cooking. All he had to do was let us eat cereal all day, and we would have been fine, but Mom gave him a fried rice recipe – boiled rice fried in a pan with diced veggies. She must have had faith in him because the recipe didn't use Minute Rice.

He could turn on the oven, a good start. Hopefully it wasn't beginner's luck. He was getting good at stirring the cooked rice in the pan with a wooden spoon. I think he surprised himself. His confidence was building, and he was really getting into it. I believe I heard him mutter to himself, "I'll show her how to cook chicken cacciatore." After a while, he stepped away from the oven and left the wooden spoon in the pan. It wasn't a plastic spoon, just a wooden spoon in contact with a hot surface. What could go wrong?

When the rice was done, he slopped some on each of our plates. Although he was proud of his creation, I don't think he was going to brag to the boys at the Post Office about how good it turned out. We gobbled up the rice even though it tasted funny. We didn't want to disappoint Dad. None of us had ever eaten rice that tasted like oak.

That wooden spoon wasn't just for Dad's cooking practice. There was a storm sewer catch basin at the corner of Hughitt and Maple streets. During heavy rainstorms, the rushing water formed a whirlpool in it. After a warm summer rain, we'd lie in it, splashing around and having a good old time. I'm sure Six Flags has fun water rides too, but I guess that water doesn't contain oil, gasoline, and antifreeze from street runoff. Big deal, if turbid pickle juice didn't harm us, neither should storm water.

One time after a rainstorm, Gene Vonn, a kid from the neighborhood, pushed Carter into the whirlpool. Mom heard Carter's cries for help, so she bolted from the house, packing the wooden spoon. Gene must have been impressed because he took off. This wasn't a paper tiger show of force; Mom wanted to teach him a lesson and followed in hot pursuit. Too bad she didn't have a big wooden fork, she could have tossed him like a salad. Mom looked like a cannibal chasing a plump treat — Run you little bastard, you'll just taste that much better. Lucky for Gene, he made it home safely. It's just as well that Mom didn't catch him; she might have ruined Dad's good rice spoon.

~~~

Soon after we moved to Iron Mountain, there was a knock on the door a few days before Thanksgiving. It was a high school girl with a box of food. Her school club was delivering food to the needy for Thanksgiving, and apparently, we were designated as needy. The girl pushed the food box at Mom, telling her we were on the list and Happy Thanksgiving.

Mom pushed back and said she appreciated the gesture, but we didn't need it. The girl wasn't buying it; she must have thought

Mom was just being proud. The girl said that we were on the list, so we were to get a box of food. Mom told her again that we didn't need it; we were all set for our Thanksgiving feast. Good thing I didn't show up at Mom's side with my finger buried in a mustard jar. That wouldn't have helped our cause. The clincher would have been Carter showing up with his hand in a pickle jar, staring at the girl with his thick glasses.

The girl dug in her heels, and, to top it off, she started to cry. "But you're on the li-i-ist!" the girl said. Now Mom was feeling sorry for her; it was a full-blown sympathy duel. What the heck, you can't keep the door open all night when it's cold outside, so Mom bowed to the list, and took the box from Miss Schindler.

Lady of Spain

Whenever we were raising hell and frustrating Mom, she would seek divine intervention. She'd close her eyes, put her hand on her forehead, and call to heaven, "Jesus, Mary, and Joseph give me strength!" We heard that prayer a lot. If anyone deserved to go out for a few drinks on Friday night, it was Mom and Dad. They'd go to the C&R Bar for fish fry and beer, their reprieve from raising ten kids. Our sitter, Jodie Baril, had fiery, sunset-red hair. In the summers, she came over after dinner and helped Mom clean the kitchen. Mom even managed to pay her a few dollars each week. In some ways, we were the only family in the neighborhood with a nanny. No one called them *au pairs*; although with all the twins it would have been appropriate. Jodie was our only sitter; maybe, she was the only teenage girl up to the task. We loved her; she was like a sister to us (sibling, not Catholic school nun).

Mom could be forgiven that if in her post-C&R revelry, she saw a bear dancing under a streetlight. Oh wait, that really happened. One Friday night when Mom and Dad returned home, they saw a bear lollygagging under the streetlight at the corner of "A" Street and Maple Street. Mom burst into the house all excited, yelling that there was a bear down the block. She called the Iron Mountain police; this was before 911, so the recording wasn't all over the news the next day. Mom told the sergeant about the bear, but he didn't believe her. "A bear?" he asked. He thought Mom was drunk. Maybe she was, but that's beside the point. She told him it was Mrs. Flaminio on Hughitt Street; then he realized it was the woman with all the kids (there, there Mrs. Flaminio, go get some rest and tomorrow the big, bad bear will be bye-bye.) The sergeant finally sent a squad car to the neighborhood, and lo and behold, the cops stumbled upon a bear. They escorted it to the City Park, nudging it along with their car horn.

Raising ten kids would leave any mother nostalgic for her carefree youth. As a teenager, Mom had played the piano accordion, an accordion with a piano keyboard. It sounds like an organ. She kept it in the closet upstairs, and every now and then, she'd take it out and sit on the bed in the girls' room, lay down sheet music, and play away. That beautiful sound would float through the house. This must have been a sight in the summer, with all the windows open, the sounds of ten kids causing trouble, accordion music, and a plastic owl tacked to the house.

Her favorite song was "Lady of Spain," also popular with hockey arena organists. There's a scene in the movie *Slapshot* where Paul Newman's character goes up to the organist, tears up the sheet music, and says, "Don't ever play 'Lady of Spain' again!"

The three brawling, hockey-playing brothers in the movie, the Hanson brothers, wore black plastic athletic glasses. Steve, Carter, and Robert wore the same kind of glasses when they played sports, and we called Carter the fourth Hanson Brother. Strangely, when his black glasses would break, he'd fix them with white athletic tape.

Two of the Hanson Brothers were actual brothers, Jeff and Steve Carlson. Before appearing in the movie, they played for the Iron Rangers, a United States Hockey League team based in Marquette, Michigan. If you liked beer and brawls (and what hockey fan doesn't), the USHL was your league. Mr. Olds, our grade school gym teacher, played for the Iron Rangers too, before the Hanson Brothers.

Lunch Lady True Confessions

In 1976, all ten of us were in school full days, so Mom took a job as a cook for the school lunch program; "hot lunch" everyone called it. They served it in the St. Mary and St. Joseph church basement, a huge space with long tables and a large kitchen with restaurant-quality ovens and freezers. You suppose that's what they mean by "cafeteria Catholics?" The church was sandwiched right between the high school and the elementary school, the perfect location.

By this time, I think every home in Iron Mountain had traded coal for natural gas because Joe the Coal Man was now the church's maintenance man. One of his side jobs was corralling the kids in the lunchroom and keeping order. This probably made him long for the row of little Flaminio heads in the window anticipating his lever pull and rumbling coal. Joe usually sat on the piano bench, while watching the kids. Some kid called him "Maestro," and the name struck a chord, so that became his name. Joe had traded black carbon for black ivory.

I don't think I'm exaggerating when I say we had the best school lunches in America. Seriously. That's what happens when an Italian, Mrs. Eutizzi, is the head cook. There cooking was so good, our high school held a lot of banquets in the church basement. Those church cellar alchemists worked magic with bulk USDA commodities. The kids on the reduced cost or free lunch program were getting quite a deal. Four stars went to the hot turkey and hot beef sandwiches. To this day, Mom still makes them for family gatherings. Sometimes, we'd have baked chicken with lump-free mashed potatoes and gravy. The spaghetti was delicious. Because the lunchroom was in the church, we were obliged to Catholic doctrine. For forty days before Easter, we'd have our traditional Lenten meatless Friday lunch of spaghetti with tuna. I didn't like it; for me it was a pass over.

Hard to believe, but some picky kids didn't like the main course, so the cooks made them peanut butter and jelly sandwiches on homemade rolls. Government peanut butter came in one-gallon metal cans stamped "USDA Peanut Butter." Federal peanut butter is quite dry, so the cooks smoothed it with vegetable oil from a one-gallon metal can stamped "USDA Vegetable Oil." Unfortunately, the Carter Administration didn't provide peanuts for the cooks to whip up "extra chunky."

For their thirteenth wedding anniversary, Dad bought Mom a diamond ring. After all she did raising ten kids, she probably qualified for a diamond every year. Lucky number thirteen. Traditionally the thirteenth anniversary gift is lace, but Dad wasn't going to be boxed in by convention. With his high-octane fertility, maybe a more appropriate gift for Mom would have been something to keep Dad at arm's length, like mace.

At hot lunch one day, Mom wiped her brow with the back of her hand. Something wasn't right; her ring finger felt lighter. She had a sinking feeling in her stomach as she pulled her hand down to take a look. It was her worst fear come true; the diamond was gone. It had come off when she was doing the dishes or preparing the vegetable tray. A diamond in the roughage! Some kid probably ate Mom's karats.

Mom knew she had to tell Dad, and she felt awful, thinking about the hard-earned money Dad had saved up for the ring. In a family of our size, that had been some act of financial acrobatics. Dad was upset at first, but it passed. Presumably, the diamond did too.

Even though Mom was cooking, cleaning, and feeding ten kids at home, working at hot lunch, and moonlighting with Dad at his janitor job, she still took a job cleaning the church. So after slinging hash in the basement, she went upstairs, vacuumed the carpeting around the altar and wiped off the Jesus statue. Hopefully when she cleaned Jesus, she didn't leave a residual liquid cleaner on his face lest some unsuspecting worshipper confuse Formula 409 with a miracle. The confessionals needed to be cleaned, too. The screen between the priest and the parishioner collected a lot of dust and lint, especially during a sin drought. The confessionals had separate doors for the priest and the sinner. A little red light above the evildoer's door turned on when the booth was occupied. No buzzer went off though when you confessed a cardinal sin. Mom's church cleaning duties didn't include trouble-shooting a malfunctioning red light because there were no electrical wiring articles in *Good Housekeeping.*

Mom also had a stint teaching Catholic CCD classes, the Confraternity of Christian Doctrine or catechism. It's the once-a-week religious instruction for Catholic kids in the public schools. The students at the Catholic school didn't have to take CCD because they lived it every day. The little old lady down Hughitt Street, Miss Musik, was Steve's CCD teacher, and one of his classmates forgot her name, so he just called her, "Miss Sing." Close enough. CCD's mission is to teach kids about the Catholic faith and prepare them for the sacraments of First Communion, Penance (confession), and Confirmation. Traditionally, the bishop confirmed the Catholic youth in Upper Michigan in the eighth grade. Because Confirmation was the culmination of CCD education, most students "dropped out" after confirmation and didn't attend during high school. The dropout rate must have lead to spiritual delinquency, so in a classic "gotcha" maneuver, the Church moved confirmation to the junior year in high school.

Mom later took on the job of coordinating all the CCD classes for the parish. She was constantly on the phone asking parishioners if they would teach a class. It always seemed to be a scramble to get enough teachers; and, of course, in a pinch, Mom would still teach.

Even with all the paying and non-paying jobs on her plate and a house full of kids, Mom thought, "You know, I have a little free time on my hands," so she served on the parish council for a few terms. It was an elected position, and I can't remember if there was some good old-fashioned Chicago-style ballot box stuffing for her victory. One night she came home from a council meeting with a list of prayers for the parishioners. One prayer was for single women in our church who were looking for a husband— "Dear St. Anne, send me a man, as fast as you can." How can you not laugh at that? We sure did. Who knows, maybe a wedding I later served as altar boy was an answer to that *haiku*.

Cooking in the basement of the church, cleaning the altar upstairs, teaching and running the CCD program, and serving on the parish council — Who says there's no place for women in the Catholic Church? Mom's done so much for Catholicism that she could cash in all her bingo chips now, never go to Mass again and still be way ahead of a lot of people.

Lord Byron, I Presume

Mom was a creative folk artist and in the 1960s, she painted on a flexible canvas a picture of Mary holding baby Jesus and trimmed it with scissors along their contours. It was her version of *Madonna and Child,* but I don't think there were any hidden codes in the art work. Every Christmas season, she tacked it to the porch door in the living room. It's still a Holiday display in Mom and Dad's home. Mary and Jesus have wavy, blond hair and pinkish-hued white skin. Jesus of Nazareth evolved into Jesus of Stockholm. That's artistic license.

One Christmas, Mom built a snow and ice amphitheater for an outdoor display of the artwork. It was just like Grandpa Jack's bathtub Madonna, only Mom's bathtub was one balmy day away from disintegrating. Mom tacked the Scandinavian Mother and Savior onto some wood, propped it inside the igloo, and put a little spotlight in front of it to illuminate it at night. She must not have had time to make the three wise kings — Bjorn, Sven and Lars — following the North Star on their reindeer.

Mom also made dried floral arrangements using weeds (weedal arrangements?). In her typical fashion, she probably saw this in a store or a magazine and said, "I can do that." She also pressed flowers between pages of books, or maybe those were just her bookmarks; I can't remember.

We called them "Mom's weeds." Even she referred to them as "my weeds." If we were riding in the car with Mom, we had to buckle down for a white knuckle screeching halt if she spotted roadside weeds that might look good dried. Her favorite was baby's breath, the aroma engulfed the house in the summer. Actually, it was nice, way better than fried burgers. She'd bundle the weeds and hang them to dry all over the house, but the front porch was her favorite spot. We'd tell our friends, "Mom's drying her weed in the front porch." She even sold some of her "weeds" at a consignment store.

We stored all kinds of things on the front porch — weeds, radio tubes, Christmas chocolates, Kathy's sort-of-cake. Once we had a jar of green swamp water on the porch. I don't know why, maybe it was habitat for a tadpole or some other vermin. John must have thought the pond juice was Mountain Dew, because he chugged it. A worried Mom called Dr. Klingler with another of John's *Guinness Book of World Records* consumption-related emergencies—from eating radio tubes to drinking swamp water. The doctor must not have been too concerned because he told Mom not to worry; he probably told her keep an eye on John to see if he grows scales.

Besides wardrobe shopping, Mom liked rummage sales for the chance to stumble across second-hand treasures. One thing about Mom, when she came across rummage sale bounty she always erred on the side of priceless.

Her biggest heist was a book by Lord Byron, the English poet from the 1800s. One page in the middle of the book had only his autograph. I have to admit, it looked authentic; I thought she'd hit a home run. This book was way too valuable for pressing daisies.

The sheet with Lord Byron's autograph was after a blank page of fragile white paper, like tracing paper. Tracing paper is used to duplicate a drawing or design. For instance, if someone wanted to copy their doctor's signature for a fake prescription, they could use tracing paper. If Mom had brought home a baseball with Lord

Byron's signature, I would have been suspicious, but this was a book. Why would the bookmaker go through the trouble of protecting the autograph behind white tracing paper if it wasn't real? After her adrenaline rush wore off, she called our kindergarten teacher, Mrs. Trembath, for her opinion. Who better to authenticate rare Victorian literature than the kindergarten teacher in Iron Mountain, Michigan? I don't think Mrs. Trembath was able to shed any light on the book, but she did tell Mom all her kids were good at their ABCs.

It wasn't just secondhand treasure that Mom over-appraised. One day, she noticed the sky bathed in orange and red; a huge fire was raging out of control somewhere west of Iron Mountain. This had to be a blaze of Biblical proportions because there was no smoke; maybe it was a big forest fire by the airport. Mom, Moomer, and Tony jumped in the car to chase it. A sky in this portion of the color spectrum was no sailor's delight. This was Dante's Inferno.

They headed out on Hughitt Street, sped into Kingsford and onto Woodward Avenue, traveling west towards the road's end at the airport. The closer they got, the more excited they became. When they drove down the hill right before the airport, they couldn't believe their eyes. Before them was the most beautiful, brilliant sunset they had ever seen.

Mom smarted from that one. After eons of getting fooled, it looked like Mother Nature won this round. Mom wasn't going to let this be the final word, so she plotted her revenge. She incubated a comeback that lasted longer than the gestation time of her six conceptions.

Years later, when Tony and Moomer were in high school, Mom flew into the house yelling, "The high school's on fire. The high school's on fire. There are fire engines everywhere!" Shocked, Tony and Moomer hopped in the car and tore east down "B" Street to the high school. Fires to the west were false alarms, but fires to the east had to be the real thing.

"Oh my God, the school's on fire," Moomer cried as they raced down the street. As they got closer, they didn't see any smoke. They didn't see any fire engines. There was no commotion. Tony asked Moomer what day it was. "April first," she said.

...And Church on Sundays

We were pretty decent Catholics growing up. We didn't attend the Catholic school in town, but 91.7% of our family went to church every Sunday (or Saturday), for the most part. Iron Mountain has a large Catholic congregation with two parishes, St. Mary and St. Joseph's on the west side (our church) and Immaculate Conception on the north side.

Two parishes merged to form our church. St. Joseph's church was destroyed in a fire in 1930, and the rebuilding left the parish with an elegant, stone church and a large debt. St. Mary's church was destroyed by fire in 1938. With St. Mary's need for a new place of worship and St. Joseph's lingering debt, the parishes combined and became St. Mary and St. Joseph's. In 2003, a fire (caused by faulty wiring) gutted most of the interior of the church. Mom did a lot of jobs in the church, but like I said, electrical wiring wasn't one of them.

The Immaculate Conception Church is a beautiful sandstone structure listed on the National Historic Register. It's reminiscent of Renaissance churches in Italy and its official Italian name is *Maria Santissima Immacolata Di Lourdes*. It was built in 1902 under the direction of Father Giovanni Pietro Sinopoli, the priest, architect, and construction supervisor. A Catholic multitasker just like Mom. Stone masons and volunteer labor from the parish, mostly Italian immigrant iron miners, built the church. They used horses to haul sandstone from a quarry one mile away and completed construction in only six months.

The first Sunday Mass in our parish was at eight a.m., for the inspired or adults who weren't out late Saturday night. I rarely went to this Mass; I didn't want to get up at seven-thirty on Sunday morning. The other services were at ten and eleven-thirty, and if a parishioner wanted a Sunday to his or herself, there was the 5:15 Mass on Saturday afternoon. When it came to church services, our parish was pro-choice.

The eight o'clock Mass had no choir and was a quick service, "the early bird special." The ten o'clock Mass was the longest because it had the adult choir. The children's choir sang at eleven-thirty; that Mass was quicker than the ten o'clock and allowed me to sleep in; it's the one I usually went to.

Only Steve, Robert and I were altar boys. At our church, one went through the altar boy training, and if he could tell the difference between water and wine, he was good to go. No pinning ceremony or hazing involved. The hardest part of serving Mass was "playing" the brass xylophone. This one was a lot bigger and more important than the multi-colored Fisher Price model at our house. During the communion rites at the altar, Father would first raise the communion wafer (body of Christ) and then the wine chalice (blood of Christ). When he offered each, the kneeling altar boy answered by banging on the xylophone with a cloth-wrapped mallet.

The xylophone had five metal chimes, progressively larger from left to right. Each chime had a different tone, and there was a specific order to tapping them during the ceremony. Someone should have showed me. After Father completed the "This is the body of Christ," ritual, I'd hammer at the chimes in left-to-right order, putting sour faces on some of the parishioners. I repeated this after he offered the blood of Christ, and I wasn't the only tone-deaf server who did it this way. (If they'd let me bring the Fisher Price, I could have answered with "Twinkle, Twinkle, Little Star," but nooo...) I think the parish finally got tired of hearing karaoke xylophone during Mass. They started using altar bells (or Sanctus bells). This is a small hand-held bell set, which was hard to screw up. Sometimes, I'd ring them a little while longer just to see how far I could push it and maybe get a glance from Father.

Right before the xylophone solo, four ushers walked to the front of the pews with the collection baskets, two up the center aisle between the two sets of pews and one at each end aisle. They walked in unison, and when they got to the front, they'd genuflect on one knee, turn around, and start collecting. It was an impressive synchronized routine, as if they had honed it with a lot of practice— Ladies and Gentlemen, put your hands together for the Genuflections!

The baskets were on long poles, ensuring that people in the middle of the pew could drop money in the basket. The ushers passed the basket in front of each person, and if he or she didn't have money, they avoided eye contact with the collectors and gazed forward. The ushers got the hint. Back then the church gave parishioners collection envelopes with a denomination check-off for their donation amount, say five, ten, or twenty dollars. I think the highest denomination check off was the Gold Captain level. Maybe I'm confusing it with Amway.

Mom always made it a point to drop something in the basket each week, even if it was only a few dollars. Although we were squeezing as much as we could out of every dime, she always made sure there was something for the Church. Dad never put money in the collection basket at church, not because he was stingy but because he was never there. In the last few decades though,

Dad has decided to relive his basic training days and now doesn't miss a Sunday Mass. He's even a card-carrying member of the Genuflections. When the ushers finished collecting, they met in the back of the church to combine the money. They'd flip over their baskets and shake them down into a nice leather box with decorative religious carvings. Sometimes we would hear coins clanging and a few of them dropping on the floor. Those must have been the days when the frugal, little old lady Angie Godin was at Mass.

After the service, the ushers brought the box to the sacristy, the room behind the altar. This was where the priest and altar boys waited before Mass; it was kind of like a locker room before game time. The altar boys still had a few small chores to do once Mass was finished. After snuffing out the candles and refilling the water and wine cruets, we straightened out the altar area to make sure everything was nice and tidy for the next service. The last order of business was skimming 10% of the cash from the leather box and putting it in an envelope for Father. Only kidding! Only kidding!

After the housekeeping, we went to the rectory refrigerator for a candy bar. Not those little Halloween candy bars, but the full size Snickers and Milky Ways, which were kept in the refrigerator. They stayed nice and cold. I thought that was odd, putting candy bars in a refrigerator; however, years earlier, a priest said, "I thought that was odd, baptizing in front of a refrigerator." Candy bars in cold storage implied no one would eat them for a while, an impossibility in our house.

Every altar boy was versed in the Divine Proportion — one Mass equals one candy bar. We all adhered to it, especially in a house of God. Well, almost everybody. Once after one of my friends and I grabbed our candy bars, we were walking away from the refrigerator when he stopped and held up his finger, not the "Thank you Jesus" touchdown finger but the "wait a minute" finger. He went back and grabbed another candy bar, stuck it in his pocket, walked a few steps, did the same finger point, and went back to repeat the chocolate thievery. I was bound by the altar boy code of silence to not say a thing. We left the rectory, me with my one Snickers bar, and he with his pockets full of them and good material for his next confession.

On special occasions, the priest performed an incense-burning ritual. The rising incense smoke symbolizes the prayers of the faithful rising up to heaven. The incense was small grains of spices and aromatics (it reminded me of birdseed), which were kept in a little metal cup with a lid, called the boat. I pictured it in the rectory when not used at Mass, full of sugar, the priest using it for his coffee while reading the newspaper. The metal incense burner (the thurible) looked like a fancy, spoutless teapot with holes. A chain fastened to the top of the thurible ran through the center of the lid, allowing the lid to slide up the chain. The lid had a porcelain knob on top that didn't get hot. The altar boy placed a small disk of black charcoal that looked like a tiny hockey puck inside the thurible and lit it beforehand, so it was hot enough to burn the "spice" and billow smoke for the ceremony.

We grabbed the knob and slid the lid up the chain with our right hand and lifted the thurible by the lower part of the chain with our left hand, so the priest could spoon in the aromatics. Hot, strawberry-red charcoal equals hot metal. One time when I slid the top up the chain, it didn't take long for my pain receptors to tell me the inside of my right index finger was pressing on the hot metal lid. Believe me, that metal was hot; hot enough to cook one of my brother Steve's upside down cheeseburgers. The priest didn't seem to be in a hurry, if the recipe called for one teaspoon of spice, he was definitely seasoning "by feel." As he looked at me with my blank stare and my eyes filling with tears, he must have thought, "Wow, Tom must really be moved by the incense ceremony." It seemed like an eternity before he was done and I could put the lid back and hand him the thurible. Like a good altar boy I toughed it out and tried to ignore the searing pain on my finger. That episode should have gotten me out of ten years of confession.

A few days later, I inspected the huge, fluid-filled blister on my finger. I couldn't help but think, hey, it wasn't *me* who stole those candy bars. A burn that "minor" wasn't enough to warrant medical attention in our family. Besides cold tap water (abundant and low-cost), a home herbal remedy would have been appropriate. What topically applied gift of nature could have alleviated the dermal trauma caused by a burning, hot cauldron of incense? Peppermint.

Field of Weeds

The Louie Mosca family lived kitty-corner from us across Maple Street. Louie had been a tail gunner on a bomber in World War II. They were good people, like everyone in the neighborhood. The Mosca kids, Larry and Laura, were a few years older than us, and one summer day they held a little "carnival" for the neighborhood kids in the vacant lot next to their house. The field was overgrown with knee-high weeds and grass. In reality, it was a carnival for the Flaminio's; however, if it had been a real carnival, we could have been the freaks. There were no rides, just some games and contests, more like a mini-Olympics with ball-throwing and jumping contests— stuff like that. Carter probably won most of the events; too bad this was well before he adopted his victory song "I couldn't sleep at all last night!" I think he took us aside beforehand saying, "I'm gonna win these games, got it?" Then he walked away, and we mocked him with a behind the head fist-cock.

One day Mr. Mosca was standing at his garage and called me over. I scooted across Maple Street, and he handed me a big, old rifle. I think it was a World War II M-1 Garand rifle, but I didn't know it at the time. Louie knew us well enough not to give me an old grenade. I don't know what ever happened to that thing. Knowing us, we probably used it as a baseball bat, maybe swinging at Hummels with it.

The Mosca kids had a small playhouse, and they gave it to us when they outgrew it. If we could count on the Mosca's for anything, it was rifles and playhouses. We plopped that little house in our yard, not quite sure what to do with it. We sat on the roof a few times, but that wasn't as much fun as the roof on the back part of our house. One muggy summer night, Carter, Robert, and I camped out in it, our bachelor pad. Unfortunately, a horde of mosquitoes wanted bachelor blood and we wound up back inside our house.

~~~

Jim had a tendency to "find" money in all kinds of places, like Mom's purse. However, he was also creative enough to make money materialize out of thin air. The only props he needed were Moscas' field and a plastic jug. One afternoon, he sat in the field pulling up weeds and grass and shoving them into the jug and then dropping in a few dollar bills he "found." He went home and showed Mom the jug of weeds and, acting confused, asked Mom to look inside. She said she didn't want to. That should have raised a red flag with Jim, because Mom's first reaction wasn't to inspect the weeds for their drying and arranging potential.

Impatient, Jim looked inside for her and to his surprise, pulled out a dollar bill. "Look, a dollar" he said excitedly. He reached in again and yelled "Another one!" Ah yes, the old Bernie Madoff maneuver. I don't think this is how boys got points towards a Boy Scout merit badge. His presentation needed work. Mom just rolled her eyes. She had watched from the kitchen window the whole time he was stuffing the jug.

Inspired by the 1976 Olympics high jumpers, I set up a high jump pit in Moscas' field, planting the seeds for my future spot on the U.S. Olympic high jump team. If that failed, since I had the proper testosterone levels, Plan B was the East German women's team. For my landing pit, I stuffed garbage bags with weeds and grass. It took longer than expected; I really could have used Jim's help. All I needed now was the high jump bar, or in my case a high jump rope. I stuck two sticks in the ground about eight feet apart and tied a rope end to each stick, about three feet off the ground. Hey, you have to work your way up. I think the weeds, sticks and rope method was the same training regimen for the Albanian high jump team—Why you take my weeds. I need for donkey! I was building my background story. Someday, I'd tell ABC Sports about the sacks of weeds for one of those "up close and personal" video segments on Olympic athletes. All I needed was an illness to overcome, like the flu, so they could recount the story with soft piano music.

After a few high jumps, some of my brothers and other kids from the neighborhood joined in. How often did you see kids playing a corner game of high jump? We were having a good time, but then the luster wore off. Landing on those bags didn't feel so good either, especially when the grass and weeds were beat down. The video crew from ABC Sports could save their tape, and we left our bags of weed in the field for Mr. Mosca.

It Came Upon a Midnight Clear

In 1973, Comet Kahoutek rocketed into the inner solar system; its trajectory clipped the earth's orbit over the Christmas holiday. Kahoutek was hyped as the "comet of the century"; a spectacular display was anticipated and earthlings cheered the galactic rock chunk and its U-turn around the sun. Rah! Rah! Rah!

Not everyone was doing the splits though. Every time a comet or other rare astronomical object appear, the doomsday kooks come out of the woodwork. Kahoutek was especially "kookish" because it coincided with Christmastime. In the 1970s, the U.S.-Soviet nuclear arms race was at its peak, so anything associated with "doomsday" got your attention. I read a newspaper article about the minister of some fringe religion claiming Kahoutek signaled the end of the world, and the comet was really a spacecraft that would land on earth on Christmas Eve. He would pilot the comet with his followers on board to the safety of outer space while those left behind perished. I didn't believe it (completely), but kept up to speed on developments, especially seat availability. I actually looked out the upstairs hallway window at night to check for Kahoutek. I asked Mom and Dad about this crazy comet cult, and they just laughed.

On Christmas Eve, we went to Midnight Mass, which at our church was ten p.m. Hey, it's midnight somewhere. Maybe this was our last night on earth, so I was thinking a little bit about Kahoutek. OK, maybe a lot about it. During Mass, I was supposed to be reflecting on the bright star signaling the birth of our Savior, but instead I was worried about a comet. At least I was thinking about a celestial body. Of course, nothing happened, and as we left church I said to Dad, "I guess that guy was wrong about the comet." I think I said that for myself more than anything. So with the bounce of a survivor in my step, I skipped back to our car to head home for some Christmas Eve festivities. I was basking in the glow of my two Christmas miracles — Comet Kahoutek didn't herald end of the world and Dad had actually gone to church.

The comet must have inspired Mom because she gave us a telescope for Christmas. Deep down, I think Mom took to heart the Johnny Cash song in the commercial about the father getting his son a Lionel toy train — "I'll never tell him that it's really mine." It was an inexpensive telescope from Sears. About three feet-long and three-inches in diameter, it was a just a white cardboard tube with lenses. If I had to describe it, I'd say it looked like a giant tampon applicator. What the ...? Oh, my God, Carter was right!

The telescope had a tripod we never used; we just held it up to our eye like a spyglass. That was a funny sight, kids holding up a telescope almost as big as themselves. I wonder how many times Angie from across the street looked out her window right down the barrel of an oversized cardboard tube. Hey, Angie, you should really get that mole checked.

One winter night, I was walking home from a friend's and saw Mom outside with the telescope. She wasn't in the yard though. She had lifted up the window sash in the girls' upstairs bedroom and was straddling the sill, one foot in the bedroom and one foot on the house extension roof under the window. Her torso was outside the window, and she held the telescope up to her eye, scanning the starry sky. Winter is a great time for star gazing; the dry, cold air really makes them twinkle. I think she was hoping for one last look at Kahoutek before it sling-shotted to some distant nebulae. Since time immemorial, man has gazed into the heavens for a release from day-to-day duties and obligations. Did I hear Mom yell into the dark starry night, "Calgon, take me away!"?

Put It on Our Bill

Irene Pascoe, a little old lady in her seventies, operated Pascoe's Store, a tiny neighborhood grocery a few blocks from our house. The store was just the front part of her house, separated from her home space by a curtain. The curtain was usually pulled to the side, so you could see into her living room. There was a big 7-Up sign in the front yard, and I don't remember swallows nesting underneath it. Too bad we never made the connection.

Pascoe's had an antique glass display case for the penny candy. I can imagine Angie Godin working behind the same case at her family store in the early 1900s. There was only enough room in Pascoe's for a candy case, a small freezer for Popsicles, Eskimo Pies and ice cream sandwiches, a few shelves for some dry goods and a meat counter. The freezer had two small top doors. When we opened them in the summer, cold, frosty air blasted out. Sometimes we'd get lucky and there'd be Dreamsicles inside, Popsicles with a creamy filling.

We'd usually go to Pascoe's with a dime or a quarter, a paycheck from doing chores for Angie. Poor Mrs. Pascoe. Kids went in there with a few pennies and took forever looking over the candy, getting fingerprints and nose prints all over the display case glass. They finally picked their candy, one piece at a time. You'd rarely see little kids happier than when they were walking out of Pacsoes, clenching in their fist a little brown paper bag full of sweets with red licorice rope sticking out.

I liked watching this little old lady put a big tube of bologna on the electric meat slicer and listening to the whirring sound of the spinning blade as she moved the meat back and forth, the slices collecting on the stainless steel pan like a deck of cards. Sometimes, she'd even toss a kid a piece, free samples just like today. She'd scoop the sliced bologna off the pan and weigh it on the scale; more often than not, she was right on. She wrapped it in brown butcher paper and tied it with a string. This was our favorite bologna, it was much better than the packaged brands.

Like most adults in the '70s, Mom and Dad smoked cigarettes. The offices on my paper routes had exhaled nicotine fumes with good hang time and ashtrays overflowing with snuffed butts. Dad smoked Viceroy and Mom smoked Salem. When it comes to soda and nicotine, people are loyal. Later, Dad switched to Marlboros because real men smoke cowboy cigarettes. Whenever they were low on smokes, they'd send us to Pascoe's. If an eight- or nine-year-old kid tried to buy cigarettes today, social services would be at the front door with a battering ram. When we'd leave for the store, they'd say, "Tell Mrs. Pascoe to put it on our bill." Mrs. Pascoe was very generous with our in-store credit; we were like Wimpy on the *Popeye The Sailor* cartoon — I'll gladly pay you on Tuesday for some nicotine today. Even though Mrs. Pascoe ran a very small operation with a razor-thin profit margin, she knew we couldn't always pay cash, so she let us pony up when we could. She did that for a few families. "Put it on our account, Mrs. Pascoe," we'd say as she handed us a pack of smokes. Then she'd pull out her little waitress pad and thumb through to the ticket full of Flaminio entries and add another one.

My sister Kathy and her friend Roberta Pancheri were in Pascoe's one day when a boy a few years older sat on the counter by the slicer. He was wearing gym shorts, and back then they lived up to the name; they were short. Unfortunately, he wasn't wearing underwear. Let's just say the meat on Mrs. Pascoe's slicer wasn't the only salami Kathy and Robbie saw in the store that day. Poor Kathy and Robbie, the Powers-That-Be haunted them with male anatomy. Another time, they were playing outside Robbie's house when a guy drove up, called them over and exposed himself. After their startled looks, he hit the accelerator and tore out of there, revving the four-stroke engine. They ran into Robbie's house and told her Mom, but not before getting the license plate number. That guy was cocky because he drove by again a little later. This time the cops showed up in a flash and arrested him a little while later.

The Landsee family lived kitty-corner from Pascoes. Bob Landsee was in Carter's class and later played offensive line for the University of Wisconsin and the Philadelphia Eagles. A shoulder injury ended his NFL career after three years. The Landsees had a big dog called Penny. I don't know what kind it was; to me it was just a blonde German shepherd. They were on my *Milwaukee Journal* paper route. One day, I knocked on the door to collect my money and when Mrs. Landsee opened the door, I saw Penny right behind her. Usually, she was outside. Why was my heart racing right then? She was eyeing me up, too. Penny, not Mrs. Landsee. An adrenaline rush cascaded through my body. Fight or flight, flight wins hands down. Sure enough, the dog bolted past Mrs. Landsee and right for me. I was Penny's candy. I screamed, grabbed the top of the stair railing, and cart wheeled over the side. Penny lunged and scratched my ankle, drawing a little blood and a lot of laughter from Mrs. Landsee. I think she was more amused by the scream than the gymnastics. Mrs. Landsee called the dog back in and paid for her paper. Condor and Dad, Penny and me. What is it with Flaminios delivering print media and German shepherd attacks? I licked my wounds and went to Pascoe's, hoping Mrs. Pascoe would toss me a slice of sympathy bologna.

Kids Get in Free

We lived across Hughitt Street from the Iron Mountain Mountaineer football stadium. That venue occupied a lot of our time all the way through high school and not necessarily for sporting events. Mom liked it because she could shoo us over there to clear the house. When *The Price is Right* ended, Bob Barker reminded everyone to get their pets spayed or neutered. That was Mom's cue to tell us to scram, even if there was no football practice or games, like in January. I always wondered if Mom and Dad purposely bought a house near the stadium, knowing it would be a good place to keep us out of mischief (sort of).

The stadium is still there and is an impressive structure for a high school. Built in the 1920s, it has eight-foot tall concrete walls around the perimeter and it encompassed a few blocks. Granted, they weren't Manhattan-size blocks, but it enclosed the playing field, running track, stands, practice fields, and the locker room, so it was big, especially to a kid. Every ten feet or so along the wall is a concrete pillar, a little taller than the wall with a pyramid top. They look like obelisks at Roman landmarks, a fine example of which is the Flaminio Obelisk in the *Piazza del Popolo* in Rome. The home stands on the Hughitt Street side were also concrete and rose to a height of about twenty feet. From the top, you could look down to the sidewalk along the street. The visitors' bleachers on the opposite side of the field were wood benches on metal framing. The home and visitor seating were removed in the 1990s and replaced with one set of stands on the home side. There are two entrance gates on Hughitt Street, one near our house and one at the other end of the block. The decorative iron gates have spires capped with a *fleur de lis*, the New Orleans Saints' symbol. A set of double gates swing open for vehicles, and on each end of the double-gate is a concrete pillar and a single gate for pedestrians. The gate profile looks like the Golden Gate Bridge.

High school seniors Steve Mariucci and Tom Izzo and their classmates painted the stadium walls yellow, since the Mountaineer colors are yellow and black. The official colors are gold and black, but in reality it's yellow and black. I remember Izzo and Mariucci sitting on a scaffold hung over the top of the concrete stands and stenciling "HOME OF THE MOUNTAINEERS" the entire length and then painting the letters black.

Steve Mariucci's and Tom Izzo's stories are well-known. They were best friends, and one went on to coach the San Francisco Forty-Niners and Detroit Lions (Mariucci) and the other (Izzo) went on to coach the Michigan State Spartans basketball team. We thought they and their teammates were larger than life. True, we were Green Bay Packer fans, but Green Bay was a whole one hundred miles away. These living legends played in the stadium right across the street, and we got to see them twice a day in August during football practice. We were as much a fixture of two-a-day practices as the tackling dummies and late summer heat.

Late one afternoon when they were done painting, I gladly helped with cleanup and lugged a loose-lidded can of yellow paint. I fumbled it and basted my shirt and pants a curry chicken color. I knew I'd be in trouble when I got home. But what luck, mustard-yellow paint. My clothes were usually stained that color anyway so no one would notice anything out of the ordinary. I could just

toss them in the chute and forget about it. However, sooner or later someone would have to do "the clogged chute stomp" on paint-soaked clothing — that would have left footprints all over the floors. Dad wouldn't have been too happy with that:
"What the hell are these foot prints?"
"Uh, that's when you were weak and God carried you?"

My brother Steve was kind of the Mountaineer team mascot in the early '70s, and the football players called him "teeny bopper." I didn't know what it meant; all I knew was if the high school football players gave you a nickname, it meant you were cool. He even had a Mountaineer letterman jacket with the cream-colored leather sleeves and black wool body. Mom sewed onto the jacket an Iron Mountain letter that a neighbor gave Steve; it was an "I" superimposed though the middle of an "M." One game night, Steve and I went to the top row of home stands before kickoff. We liked going up there to pass time, looking over the edge and spitting on the sidewalk. Once the game started, Steve told me he was going down to the sidelines and left me in the stands. He just walked out onto the field and took a seat on the team bench; no one stopped him. It was as if an usher had opened the velvet ropes for this kid and showed him to his seat.

The Mountaineer varsity played their home games on Saturday nights, the junior varsity and freshmen on Thursday nights. One thing was certain; Flaminio's didn't pay to get into games. It was our way of trimming the fat from the household expenses. I'm sure everyone associated with Mountaineer football knew we didn't part with what few coins we had in our pockets on Thursday and Saturday nights. This was made perfectly clear to Robert at the ticket booth across the street from our house.

The booth, next to the pedestrian gate, was a small, wooden shack behind the concrete wall. Fans on the sidewalk paid through a window cut into the concrete. The window had vertical iron jail bars, and you slid your money and received your tickets from the attendant. Those bars are still there today. In big cities, they use protective Plexiglas in ticket booths, in Iron Mountain, steel bars. Just like a wild West train depot ticket booth, apparently Iron Mountain had roving bands of thieves on horseback looking for a quick score.

When the athletic director, Mr. Butler, was in the booth setting up for a game Robert walked over asked, "How much does it cost to get into a game?"

Mr. Butler barked at Robert with his loud booming voice, "Of course you don't know how much it costs, you Flaminio's never pay!"

How true. Let it be said though that Mr. Butler was a good guy and very good to us. When we were older, he'd give us made-up jobs, so we could make some money — jobs like handing the opposing football team's coach the key to the visitors' locker room at the high school a mile away. That's a tough job only one of us could handle.

Mr. Butler was a gym teacher too, and in junior high school, we played Wiffle ball in the gym while he umpired from a bench as he read *The Chicago Tribune*. He'd hold the paper up in front of his face, oblivious to the game; there were no cutout viewing holes in the paper. For a call needing an umpire's decision, someone would yell, "Mr. Butler, was he out or safe?" Without even looking out from behind the paper, he'd just say, "He was out," and make a quick sign with his thumb without missing a beat of Mike Royko's column.

Mr. Butler bore the burden of proof for his accusation about Flaminio admission price ignorance. Our sneaking-in *modus operandi* had different flavors, just like pudding. We rotated our methods, so we didn't get complacent and slip up. One maneuver was "The Ambulance Entrance." The ambulance parked behind the west end zone and entered the stadium before game time through the double gate at that end. We'd hang around outside, waiting for the meat wagon to show up, ready to make our move. Sometimes we'd wear a sad face, hoping a ticket taker would take pity and admit us free. However, this was not as much fun as sneaking in. This Oliver Twist tactic had a low success rate anyway.

When the ambulance arrived, the stadium workers opened the gate. The ambulance slowly drove in right past the ticket taker, standing along the passenger side. The trick was to walk right in step with the ambulance, on the driver side, so the ambulance was a buffer between us and the nameless, faceless ticket taker. We walked in line with the rear tires in case he looked under the ambulance. Sometimes, success depended on the person who opened the gate. If he understood that we didn't pay to get in, he might look the other way.

Once Robert, Carter and I were loitering by the gate before a game against our cross-town rival, Kingsford, casing the joint and evaluating our options. If someone had asked us what we were doing, we would have said, "Waiting for the ambulance."

Iron Mountain and Kingsford are separated by Woodward Avenue and the football game between the two schools is the biggest event of the year. The week leading up to the game is always full of all sorts of shenanigans, like egg throwing and other juvenile vandalism.

In a rare twist, before this particular Kingsford game, our neighbor Clyde, who'd set up the yard line markers, told us we could go in, but under one condition: we had to sit on the Kingsford side. Apostasy! We'd be stuck the entire game rooting for Iron Mountain on the Kingsford side. Sure, maybe we could wander over to the Iron Mountain side to the concession stand for a hot dog, but then our oath to Clyde would oblige us to head right back to the dark side. I was certain he'd be checking up on us at least once every quarter to make sure we were still over there. We wanted no part of that; at least Robert and I didn't. Carter said, "OK," and we watched as he walked into the stadium and melted with the Kingsford fans. Probably looking back and muttering "suckers."

The two die-hard Mountaineer fans went home. Mom asked why we weren't at the game. We told her about Clyde's ridiculous terms and conditions and Carter's acceptance of said terms. "You fools," she said, "just walk over to the Iron Mountain side when the game starts and stay there." Oh, that's what Carter's plan was? Why hadn't Clyde just told us we could walk over to the Mountaineer side when the game started? Why present it as a Zen koan?

We watched a lot of games for free courtesy of "The Trojan Horse." Iron Mountain's opponent arrived before the ambulance, so this was the first option. There were usually thirty-five to forty players on the other team, throw in a few managers and water boys, and you're talking serious cover. Due to our size, we couldn't put on football uniforms for mimicry; although I'm sure if we asked, Mom would have made us replica jerseys for each team. Grandma Rahoi could have knit us pilot hat/helmets too.

The suited-up players unloaded from the bus and gathered on the sidewalk. When the gates opened, they'd enter *en masse* hooting and hollering. All we had to do was blend in with them; next thing you know, we were inside, quietly dissolving into the crowd. I could imagine someone at the gate saying, "Looks like the Flaminios are Gladstone Braves this week. I guess next week they'll be Escanaba Eskimos."

"The Bathroom" was our ace in the hole. The field house was located in the southwest corner of the stadium, and the men and women's bathrooms were on the west side of the field house, completely out of view from the rest of the stadium. The little corridor between the bathrooms and the stadium wall was like an alley, and all we'd do is scale the wall outside, jump down into the alley and, Eureka, we're in. When we were taller, we'd step off a concrete pillar base to grab the top of the wall and do a pull-up; when we were shorter, we needed a boost, or we propped a board against the wall as a step.

When our head cleared the top of the wall, the first thing we did was make sure the coast was clear. I wonder how many times someone walked back there to go to the bathroom and saw one of our heads resting on top of the wall? Move along, nothing to see here. Four of us at once would have looked like Mount Rushmore. When all was clear, we'd lift ourselves over the top and leap down. Now one of us was the lookout for the next wall monkey. We'd stagger our return from "the bathroom" to be less conspicuous. When I came from around the corner of the field house, I'd do a quick tug of my fly to sell it.

One time, outside the wall, we heard, "Hey you kids!" Uh oh, it was Rosie Vondale. The Vondale family lived on the corner of Hughitt Street and Birch Street. This was the side street that ran along the west stadium wall. Rosie was a little older than our parents, and had a salt and pepper afro; maybe it wasn't an afro, but it kind of looked like one to us. She was always sweeping her driveway; I guess it was always dusty.

We thought she was going to shoo us with her broom or have us sweep her driveway because her arms were tired. Maybe she heard through the grapevine that we worked cheap for Angie. Our fear was unfounded. "Use this," she said as she pulled a chair from her garage. All right! The first and only adult accomplice for one of our break-ins. We propped the chair against the stadium wall and scampered over under Rosie's approving eye. Since an adult helped, we wouldn't have to tell the priest about sneaking in at our next confession. I think that was a rule.

Sometimes, we would barter labor for admission. A few hours before game time, the stadium workers set up the yardage markers and end zone corner flags. The flags were on thin metal rods, so a running back diving for the corner was an eye poke away from Flaminio vision. The yard markers were thick black rubber mats with two faces that folded out like a roof on a house, one face showing the yard line number to the home side and the other to the visitor side.

The workers drove the markers onto the field in a pickup truck, and sometimes we'd just show up, start pulling them off the truck, and set them up. They never asked us to help, we just did. I'm sure at first they kind of looked at us like *What the heck are these kids doing?* But after a while, they didn't seem to mind. Usually, this took place a good two hours before game time, so after we were done, we'd just hang around until kick-off. Rule of thumb: once we were in, no one ever told us to leave.

The Tanner's house was across Birch Street from the west wall, even with the goal posts. They watched free football too from the comfort of their Chevy Impala station wagon hood. We would sit in the stands and look across the end zone and over the wall, seeing Mr. and Mrs. Tanner standing on their car watching the Mountaineers, usually with their arms folded. They were years ahead of the rooftop game watchers at Wrigley Field. Any way someone comes up with to watch a Mountaineer football game free, I say more power to them. If a field goal had gone through the uprights and over the wall, the Tanners could have caught it (after unfolding their arms). I don't know why we never joined them; we could have parked our Impala Station wagon right next to theirs and done some tailgating before the game. I wonder if our Impala roof and hood would have supported the load of our family.

~~~

One day, Steve came home from watching a practice and said quarterback Steve Mariucci had separated his shoulder and would miss the game against Escanaba the coming Saturday. Worse yet, he said it had happened when the head football coach, Mr. Gusick, tackled him. What!? Why would Mr. Gusick assault one of his best players? I was crushed. Escanaba was the best team in Upper Michigan, and without Mariucci, Iron Mountain didn't stand a chance. I even thought maybe I'd skip the game on Saturday, just stay home and save the cost of a ticket. Right. What would I be saving?

The backup quarterback was Earl Huotari, a starting defensive back who wore a number in the twenties. What quarterback wears a number in the twenties? A quarterback who doesn't expect to play quarterback, that's who (OK, maybe John Hadl of the San Diego

Chargers.) It would take divine intervention for a quarterback with a number in the twenties to lead Iron Mountain to victory. In 1974, it would take Green Bay Packer Coach Dan Devine's intervention to trade away the Packer's future for John Hadl and his number twenty-one jersey.

Of course there was no way I'd miss the game no matter who was quarterback. I was in the stadium well before the game started. It was late October, already dark, and the lights were on. The only two people on the field were Steve Mariucci and me. I was on the sidelines watching Mariucci walk right down the center of the field, arm in a sling and head down, dejected that he couldn't play. It was a pitiful scene, like one of those sappy movies from the 1930s about a fallen sports hero and his disappointed kid fan. Only in those movies, the hero fell from grace due to drinking or gambling, not felonious assault by the coach — Say it ain't so, Steve! I wonder if the Tanners were standing on their car, watching from behind the wailing wall, with their arms folded and tears slowly running down their cheeks, like the Indian when someone litters.

Well, there was no Lou Gehrig/Wally Pipp drama that night at Mountaineer Stadium. Iron Mountain lost, but it wasn't Earl's fault. Escanaba was a good team and probably would have beaten Iron Mountain even with Mariucci on the field. And Mr. Gusick did not tackle him and separate his shoulder.

Most people in Iron Mountain were Green Bay Packer fans, since Green Bay was only a hundred miles south. Every Packer fan's goal is to watch a game at Lambeau Field. One August Saturday night, Dad and his brother Jerry took Steve and me to an intra-squad scrimmage. It wasn't officially a game, but we didn't care. We wouldn't even have to sneak into the game because it was free, so the commandment that Flaminio's don't pay to watch football wasn't violated.

I was almost as excited about eating at McDonalds before the game. There wasn't a McDonalds anywhere in Upper Michigan, and the one in Green Bay was the nearest. We might as well have been going to *Gilligan's Island* for a coconut cream pie because both places were fantasylands that just existed on TV. Steve and I anxiously awaited our first Big Macs, finally finding out what was so secret about the sauce. This McDonalds was an older one with the big, single gold arch in front. When we got our Big Macs, I couldn't believe how big they were, a lot bigger than our Friday burgers. Less odorous too. Steve and I tore into them, finally getting in on the secret. We loved them. With the fries and the Coke, I soon realized I wouldn't be able to finish the Big Mac. I ate a little more than half of it and gave the rest to Steve who wolfed it down. I don't remember much about the game, but then again it was just the Packers offense against the defense. The biggest part of the trip was eating at McDonalds and becoming a real American.

Like McDonalds, black people were a rarity in the Iron Mountain area. Many people there, if they saw a black guy in town, assumed he was a Packer. Dad told me a story of an old-timer from town sitting next to a black guy on a flight from the airport in Kingsford. Their conversation went something like this:

"Do you play for the Packers?"

"No."

"What do you do?"

"I'm a doctor."

"What's your name?"

"Lemon."

"You related to the guy that plays for the Detroit Tigers?"

~~~

My only dabbling in criminal mischief involved the stadium's new concession stand. The Mountaineer Booster Club built a small wooden snack shack on the visitor's side, so the enemy fans didn't have to walk to the other side for treats. It was just plopped on the dirt ground, no foundation or flooring. Big mistake. One time Ted Doyle, another friend, and I burrowed underneath the back wall of the shack, just like badgers. We emerged from the hole looking at stacks and stacks of trays of one-quart glass bottles of Pepsi and 7-Up. Those stationary bottles were a lot easier pickings than the marching bottles on the assembly line that I'd seen in Head Start. We started grabbing bottles and chugging. Cola nut, uncola nut, we chose wisely and unwisely. We could have chugged and belched all afternoon, but now that we had an unlimited supply of soda, we didn't really want it anymore. We did the next thing we could think of, we shook the bottles with our hands over the openings to build up the carbon dioxide pressure, removed our hands and sprayed the caramel water. When that fun extinguished, we put the empty bottles back in the trays because that's the right thing to do, and scurried out the hole. The padded blocking dummies were stored behind the shack, so we covered our portal with them. We knew our free soda days were numbered, and eventually someone would see the empty bottles and figure it out.

A week or so later, I was working on the front porch roof with Dad. We'd torn down the old porch, and we were pounding roof shingles on the new one. We were hammering away when I saw Mr. Izzo's car slowly approaching on Hughitt Street. I knew it was the Izzo's car from a block away because it was a gold-bronze car with a black top. There was a sticker on the car that said "Mafia Staff Car, Keepa You Hands Off." Mr. Izzo was in the Mountaineer Booster Club. I couldn't imagine what he wanted. He stopped right in front of our house and yelled to Dad through his car window, "Hey Jim, have you seen any kids hanging around in the stadium? Someone broke into the concession stand." Everyone knew we were always in there, even when the stadium was locked, but they knew we'd never do anything bad because we were good kids, after all. I looked down and hammered furiously. Surely Dad never saw anything and Mr. Izzo would soon be on his way.

"Yeah," Dad said. "I've seen that Doyle kid hanging around in there." Great, my Dad just ratted out my accomplice and in the process nailed me. The blood drained from my face while I pounded nails like a madman. Dad must have thought to himself,

"Who's this Amish kid on the roof with me?"
Mr. Izzo said thanks and drove off. He either forgot or didn't feel like making a big deal because nothing ever came of it. My breaking and entering days were over. Luckily, it wasn't a gateway to worse crimes, except for sneaking into games.

When Tony and Moomer graduated high school, the Iron Mountain Board of Education presented Mom and Dad with a lifetime pass to Iron Mountain sporting events. There's a novel concept, Flaminios getting in free to football games. They should have just presented them with a gold ladder to climb the wall by the Vondales.

Desperately Seeking Patti McGuire

The stadium wasn't just for passing time on hot August days or watching football games. All boys reach an age when they act on their God-given duty to look at pictures of naked ladies and look at them frequently. For us that meant getting our hands on *Playboys* and Mountaineer Stadium was our book depository. We stored them in there like a squirrel hiding acorns; only, we never forgot where they were. We learned about faith between the pews and female anatomy between the goal posts.

Back in the '70s if you were our age, you had to work at it if you wanted photos of lady parts. It wasn't like today where a few key strokes to cyberspace lead you to a never-ending parade of pixelated porn. Kids today don't know how tough we had it. A full, intact *Playboy* was the crown jewel. Once we found a stack in our basement, probably left by the previous owner. I guess the magazine dates may or may not have confirmed that. One day, they mysteriously disappeared. Those people must have come back to claim them.

Sometimes, we'd get them from a teenager in the neighborhood or a friend's older brother. A lone centerfold or a few torn out pages were OK too; we could fold them and carry them in our pockets. Like most guys, we didn't bother with the articles. The only way we would have read a *Playboy* article was if it was on the back of a box of Cocoa Puffs.

When we scored a *Playboy* (or several), we had to find a good hiding place. The stadium was the best, it was nearby with a gated, locked entrance. Because we spent so much time in there, we knew every nook and cranny, just like we knew every nook and cranny of a lot of air-brushed twenty-something girls.

We had several options for hide and seek. The valve box for the sprinklers was OK when they weren't watering the field; otherwise we would get soggy centerfolds. The locker room roof? Too much work to get up there, plus we'd be easily spotted and arouse suspicion. We wanted to arouse something, but not suspicion.

The best spot was beneath the concrete home stands where a ramp in the middle led down to the tunnel underneath the stands. The track hurdles were stored in the dark, dry tunnel; they were the perfect cover. My brother Steve, some friends, and I fished some out once and sat in the sun-baked stands, each with our own out-of-date issue. Not during a football game, but on one of those hot, lazy summer days made for boys and Playboys.

The centerfold page had personal information written in black magic marker, supposedly authored by the centerfold herself, tidbits like "Tammy is into water sports, world peace and quantum physics," and some boys could rattle off the names of dozens of centerfolds and give a biography on each of them. Not me. They were forever nameless to me, their hobbies and interests immaterial.

But I never forgot Playmate Patti McGuire, the girlfriend of tennis pro Jimmy Connors. She was a beautiful young lady, and I'll always cherish the time we spent together. So the lives of Patti McGuire, Babe Ruth, and Jesse Owens intersected at Mountaineer Stadium. Too bad all three weren't there at the same time, it would have been just like *The Incredible Journey.*

So as not to be accused of being homers, we also hid some magazines underneath the visitor's bleachers. Those were just regular bench bleachers on a metal framing. We'd cover the visitor editions with an extra wood bench lying on the ground. One day, Donny Hudson and I went to the stadium to review some nooks and crannies. With no football practice or game, we had the place to ourselves. When the gates were locked, we'd just climb over. We'd always laugh when someone fumbled with a key and the gate lock, trying to get inside.

It was easiest to climb over the pedestrian gate where it connected to the pillar, the lowest part of the gate. The middle horizontal section of the gate had rings wide enough for our feet. All we did was grab onto the gate bars, step up, get one foot in one ring and the second foot in another, and pull ourselves up by the *fleur de lis* on top of the spire. We'd hold on to the concrete pillar for support and step on top of the gate; then we would reverse the process to get down on the other side. We he to be careful because the spire tips could do some serious damage. God forbid we fell on one of those; we wouldn't want to go near a centerfold for a while.

One of the vertical gate bars was bent at the bottom, widening the gap between it and the adjacent bar. Donny was the only person in the neighborhood skinny enough to go through the gap. He'd zip though the gate like a ghost going through a wall.

After I climbed over the gate and Donny crossed over as he paranormally did, we ran over to the visitor bleachers for our booty. We sprawled on the green grass behind the stadium bleachers with some beautiful girls. Just like the Van Morrison song, but not quite. We flipped through the pages and raced past the text to get to the photos. The clock stood still because we were so caught up in the moment. The sound of feet crunching on the black cinder track in front of the bleachers shattered our nirvana. We peered through the bleachers and saw it was one of the football coaches on an afternoon jog. If he saw us, he'd be sure to ask what the hell we were doing. Deflated, we put our *Playboys* back underneath the plank and waited until he was on the opposite side of the field. Then we ran the twenty yards or so to the wall behind the bleachers and scampered over.

The home stands had a walkway in front of the first row, about three feet above the running track, with a metal pipe guard railing along the walkway. A few of the vertical pipe posts weren't set in the concrete; they terminated just outside of and below the walkway. We soon discovered those posts were hollow, open at the bottom, and perfect diameter for a rolled up skin magazine. We'd just roll them up and shove them in, like loading an artillery shell in a canon — fire in the hole! We had to be careful not to push them too far in the pipe or else we'd never get them out of there, and our centerfold would forever be just a pipe dream. We'd push them in just far enough so we couldn't see them but still finger them out.

That hollow pipe was my favorite hiding spot. Out of habit, I checked it for *Playboys* long after they were gone. When I looked up in that pipe and saw nothing, the pipe wasn't the only thing that was empty. Even years later, when I was in high school track practice, I'd peek in those hollow pipes now and then, hoping against hope that Patti McGuire was keeping thè home fires burning.

~~~

Our *Playboy* stashes always vanished. Either one of our friends betrayed us, or another roving band of porno pirates abducted them. Maybe the stadium workers found them, read them, and waited for us to restock. After all, even for us, our stadium mistresses got old after awhile. The same bunnies day after day got monotonous. Except Patti McGuire, for me she was monogamous.

In the summer, we walked around the neighborhood or rode our bikes in the woods, opportunistically on the lookout for *Playboys* or torn pages from one. Every weather-beaten page on a sewer grate demanded attention. We'd pick up those wet, crumpled glossy sheets full of potential and unfold them like they were the Dead Sea Scrolls. A magazine picture can get so mangled and weather-beaten, we saw whatever body part our minds wanted us to see, like a Rorschach test (I see a boob! You're crazy, it's a basketball.)

After flattening out a wet page, we'd lay it out to dehydrate it, like we were drying chile pods in the hot New Mexico sun. Our pasta/ clothes drying rack might have been handy. As much care went into drying those pictures as went into the darkroom developing them. While it's true that water and sun will damage centerfolds, they don't do so much that our Kodak moments were ruined. I always wondered who would leave such valuable material exposed to the elements. Hadn't they heard of metal pipes? Now you can get these photos on the internet, and the only way you'll ruin them is if you drop your laptop in a mud puddle. It's true what they say; print media is dead.

Pornographic access was tough for adults too in the 1970s. Back then, the only way they could watch a porno flick was to either go to a movie theater or find someone with an eight millimeter movie projector. If they went to the theater, they had to walk under the giant marquee announcing the movie and then wave to their neighbors as they drove by and honked the horn. Maybe that's why the plastic Groucho Marx glasses and moustache were so popular.

There was something creepy about a guy owning an eight-mm movie projector; you knew he had it for one reason: skin flicks. However, it was socially acceptable to have a projector for a bachelor party because that was a special occasion. Schools always had movie projectors too, so if you knew a teacher, theoretically you could see adult movies. Not us kids, though. We got to watch movies about wildlife or the forming of the Great Lakes, preceded by a public service message from Bob Hope on a Texaco oil drilling platform.

One day, Carter and I were amblin' down a road by the Westside baseball field when he found a strip of about twenty-five frames from an eight-millimeter film. We held it up to the sky, and what luck! The strip was a topless woman with one hand on her head and the bent elbow covering her breast. The frames progressed from the "actress" slowly moving her elbow out of the way, exposing her boob. We held it into the sunlight and jerked it up and down, believing that this manual manipulation would give us a roadside matinee. I don't think this is how Steven Spielberg got the directing bug. I have no idea what the title of that X-rated movie was, but as far as this Siskel and Ebert were concerned, it was "Two Thumbs Up."

Our Zapruder moment must have given Carter the movie bug because one Christmas he got a movie projector for creep shows. He must have beaten Robert to the back page of the Christmas catalogue. We'd tack a bed sheet to the basement wall and watch abbreviated versions of movies like *The Incredible Shrinking Man* or *Tarantula.* Almost all of Carter's flicks were 1950s and '60s B-horror movies. Maybe Dad had some of his own movie reels we didn't know about. We never found any left behind by the previous homeowner.

Football, Drugs, and Money

After sweating in the summer heat, the Iron Mountain football players popped little yellowish-orange salt tablets to replenish the brine that poured from their skin. Those were the performance enhancing drugs of the day, M&M-size salt licks. One of those pills was just the sodium equivalent of a large bag of potato chips with a soy sauce chaser. The tablets came in a large plastic jug with a wide-mouth screw top, wide enough for your hand, just like a big pickle jar. I don't think the salt pills were kosher, though.

After one practice, a player gave Steve a pill, and when he came home he proudly told Mom about his salty snack. Mom wasn't happy. Who were these hippie high schoolers giving her little boy pills? What if salt pills were a gateway to another culinary pharmaceutical, like sugar cubes? She was ready to call the head coach (or in her mind, the head pusher) and let him have it. Since Steve wasn't showing any signs of reefer madness, Mom just warned him about pills and football players.

Sunday morning was just as important to us as the Saturday football game, not necessarily for church but because a lot of people in the stadium on Saturday meant a lot of people losing money. On Sundays, we'd wake up at dawn to scour the stadium for money. (Funny side note, when we were kids, Steve told me,

"Tony Orlando was kidnapped. But he's OK, he was found at the crack of Dawn.")

On Saturday night, we'd enjoyed four quarters of football action, and on Sunday morning, we hoped for four quarters in our pockets. I always went to the stadium early while there was still frost on the ground. If I got there after it had evaporated, so had the money because one of my brothers had beat me to it. I especially liked finding shiny quarters; it was sweet revenge on that garbage man who'd made a fool of me.

It wasn't a group effort; whenever we woke, we headed over there. I'd be at one side of the stadium and see someone else climbing over the gate, probably a brother. Is that Carter? No, it's Robert. We would walk around the stadium where the spectators stood, under the visitors' bleachers, and through the home stands, and then do it again. We left no empty popcorn box unturned because we never knew if one of those boxes was hiding some green. Carter's and Robert's eyes were so bad there was a good chance they missed something; retracing their steps could still pay dividends.

I think we were the only ones in the neighborhood who did this; it was as if everyone else knew not to even bother. This was our established turf, and we didn't need to tag the stadium walls with spray paint to prove it. Maybe the other kids just didn't want to get up early on a Sunday for a few coins. The stadium cleanup crew showed up later in the day, and by then we had picked the place clean. If there was any money left in there, it had to be *pesos* because every cent of American currency was in our pockets.

~~~

One afternoon, Steve barged in the house and in all seriousness announced, "I found marijuana in the stadium." Say what? First salt pills and now this? You are supposed to look for dimes in the stadium, not dime bags. How do you even know what marijuana looks like?

I was waiting for a half-baked line like "Yeah, there's grass on the football field." But no, he was serious. We had listened to our friend's *Cheech and Chong* records; maybe Steve thought that made him a cannabis expert. Dad told him to go get it to see if he knew what he was talking about. If so, then Dad would have been concerned with Steve knowing what he was talking about.

Steve and I climbed over the gate and crossed the football field to the visitors' bleachers where he had told me he found it. Oh great, the bleachers are now home to Steve's pot stash and my *Playboy* stash. We went beneath the stands, and Steve picked up a flattened popcorn box, where he'd hidden the "marijuana." He reached in and pulled out a wilted weed.

That's it? I looked around and thought, *Jeez Steve, why didn't you just pull up one of the live ones that's growing all over beneath the bleachers. You think that's some kind of hash? Sheesh, I've seen that herb growing all over the west side of Iron Mountain.*

So we headed home with Steve's jolly thyme popcorn and showed it to Dad. He took one look at it and said "That's not marijuana."

Disappointed and unconvinced, Steve called Dad's bluff. "How do you know?"

"Because I do," said Dad.

End of story.

Another time, Steve and I were at his friend's older sister's birthday party. The birthday girl got a card with some teen-ager riddles and read them aloud to see if anyone knew the answers. One brainteaser was, "What is a teen-ager's favorite fruit"?

Steve excitedly raised his hand, "I know, I know."

This was a teenage girl's birthday party, but Steve had the confidence of a returning Jeopardy champion and jumped in before any of the girls had a chance. "It's marijuana," said Iron Mountain's resident reefer expert.

Everyone in the room laughed. The correct answer was "dates."

Run, Laotian, Run!

Spring was for track and field, another season with a reason for us to be inside the hallowed walls. In some ways, track meets were a letdown because admission was free, so we missed the thrill of the break-in. We never saw the Tanner's standing on their car watching the hundred-yard dash either. Back then, all the races' distances were still in yards; the metric system wasn't accepted yet in America. Kind of like now. It wasn't until 1980 that Michigan high school track and field went metric. Well just track, not field. The long jump and shot put were still measured in English units.

It's funny, all through grade school our teachers told us to "Get ready for the metric system," because the whole world will be using it. And what happened? The only time Americans encounter it is during the Olympics and, in an ironic twist, in the illicit drug culture. Kilos and grams are part of the everyday pharmaceutical calculus. Who would have thought that stoner slackers would be the ones embracing the new math? They were told countless times they'd never amount to anything, but at least they knew one thousand grams was a kilogram. They knew you just had to move the decimal point.

The track team had all kinds of neat equipment we used without regard to manufacturer instructions. The high jump landing pits were chunks of spongy foam rubber encased in netting, about eight feet long and a few feet thick; usually, there were four or five of them at the landing area. If the pits weren't packed close together and a high jumper landed between two of them, he'd have a nice landing on the hard ground. They were bulky and had to be dragged or carried by several people. Left outside during a rainstorm, they'd get waterlogged and were even harder to move. They were comfortable as hell, and I remember lying on one during a sunny track practice and dozing off. Lucky for me, it was when the high jumpers weren't using it.

One day, we found some of the foam sausages left outside. Carter, Robert, some of our friends, and I dragged a few of them to the east end of the home stands, right in front of the concession window. Looking up, we saw about a twenty-foot drop onto the pits. There was a steel guardrail a few feet in front of the window, so we placed the sponge nets just outside of it. We each made a mental note of that rail; there were no style points for landing on it crotch first.

We took turns jumping off from the top of the stands, making sure to spring out a little bit to clear that lower guardrail next to the pits. When we were at the top, a car driver headed west on Hughitt Street would see us, so two of us would pretend-fight, and one would push the other off. I don't know where we thought up half the stuff we did.

However, all good things must come to an end. One of our friends landed on the corner of a pit, smacking his foot on solid ground. He was in a lot of pain, and that's when the track coach came over and asked us what the hell we were doing. He had pretty much figured it out. Just like in *Lord of the Flies*, adult authority intervened to rein in a tribe of kids who had lost touch with their humanity. He ordered us to drag the pits back. In this alternate universe, when a coach told you to do something, you did it, without question. This was probably one of the dumbest things we did; someone could have gotten seriously hurt. Lucky for our friend, he had no broken bones, which passed as "not hurt bad" for us.

For a few years, Iron Mountain's pole-vaulters used the same landing pits. At least they were better than the sawdust piles they used in the black-and-white era. They replaced them with "Cloud 9," a huge, white, vinyl, inflated pillow like you see kids jumping on at carnivals. It had "Cloud 9" printed on the side and a large fan to inflate it. I wonder how many guys on the track team fantasized about getting their girlfriends on that thing — Baby, with you I'm on Cloud 9.

The fan reminded me of the one on the Sacchetti's air boat; one of those low draft, flat-bottom boats powered by a huge fan on the back. That had to be the only airboat for hundreds of miles. It was good for the Florida Everglades, or the Robicheauxs of the bayou, and apparently, Mr. Sacchetti thought it was good for lakes in Upper Michigan too.

When a pole-vaulter landed on it, a thrust of air rushed out of the fan located at the end of the cloud. Nice, we can occupy our time with that. We'd crowd around the fan and wait for a vaulter to land, anticipating the airburst. If he was taking his time, concentrating on trying to clear the bar, we'd pop up our heads like prairie dogs and look over the cloud and down the runway at him — come on already! It was a good thing that 747s didn't land at the airport in town; the backwash from the jet engines would have been too tempting.

We didn't just need one hundred-fifty pounds of humanity landing on Cloud 9 to have fun. We liked to yell into the fan too because the spinning blades made our voices warble. An argument with a fan is a common occurrence in stadiums. Sometimes, we'd tempt fate and stick our fingers through the protective fan cage to see how close to the whirling blades we could get. Maybe that's why Joe Sacchetti kept us arms-length from his airboat. No worries though, there's still one hundred fingers between us.

Our time in the stadium during track meets wasn't spent solely doing improv with the equipment. We actually enjoyed watching track meets too. In 1973, an exchange student from Laos, Saikang Sisovong, attended Iron Mountain High School. His classmates just called him Sai (like "sigh"). I thought it was amazing that with all the war and strife in Southeast Asia someone from Laos was going to school here.

During one track meet, Sai lined up in his starting blocks for the hundred-yard dash and crouched in the sprinter's stance with his one knee and his fingertips on the black cinder track. The starter had his pistol in the air ready to start the race. One shot, and the runners take off, but if another shot follows, it means someone jumped the gun, and they'd have to restart. The shot rang out and Sai bolted out of the blocks. He must have been a little anxious because the starter shot again. All the runners heard the second shot except Sai; he kept running. I imagine that anyone who grew up in Southeast Asia in the 1960s and 1970s and heard "Bang bang!" had a natural reflex to run like hell. The amazing thing was that Sai ran in a straight line after the double shot. Decades earlier at a race in the stadium, it was a horse that was spooked by a gunshot, and now it was a kid from the Mekong Valley. Sai kept sprinting and his teammates cheered him on, some were on the edge of the track shouting encouragement, "Come on Sai! Come on Sai!" It kind of sounded like the "Banzai! Banzai!" that I heard in the war movies I watched. Even the people in the stands were cheering. The hundred-yard dash was run from east to west, and here was Sai, arms pumping, legs churning, and eyes squinting into the western sun. Sai broke the string at the finish line. Here he was, basking in his glory, ready to rub some Laotian into those sore, tired American sprinters. Then someone told him the bad news. As he looked one hundred yards down the track, panting and sweating from his victory, he could see the other runners and the starter, hands on their hips waiting for him. All that running for nothing. Sigh. He took it in stride and laughed. He trotted back to the start line, a lot slower than the original trip.

They restarted the race, and this time there was only one "bang" from the pistol. I'm sure Sai didn't win the do-over. At least when he went home to Laos, he could tell his friends that he was the first one to cross the finish line in a race with Americans (How many baskets of rice did you have to carry in the race?). Maybe his classmates back home used Sai's story as a source of inspiration, and in some Laotian village, there is a statue of a victorious Sai breaking the string.

Double Breast, Triple Axle

Playboys were mostly summer fun because the weather and school vacation cooperated. Post-winter solstice centerfolds were rare, but once in a blue moon, they provided warmth on a cold, winter day, just like a muff. The stadium bunnies were hibernating under the snow, and the geese "V" flying north over our house in April pointed the way to the female pelvic regions only a few warm weeks away.

There was an ice skating rink on the vacant lot outside the stadium's east wall, across Hughitt Street from Miss Musik's house. Back in the 1970s, there wasn't an indoor rink in Iron Mountain, or most towns in Upper Michigan. Only the hockey hotbeds of Houghton, Marquette, Sault Ste. Marie, and a few other scattered locations had them.

The city workers watered vacant lots around town to make ice rinks. Most kids in our hockey-clueless neighborhood wore figure skates: the boys' black and the girls' white. One of our neighbors gave us a box of figure skates when their kids outgrew them. There were boys' and girls' skates of varying sizes, so there was usually the correct size and sex to wear.

One January night Bobby Doney, Lori Vonn, Robbie Pancheri, and I were skating at the rink. Bobby and I had a *Playboy*, the boys' life. It was our backup plan when we got tired of skating, which for us wouldn't be long. A street light at the edge of the rink provided ample candle power for anatomical illumination. After a few skate-arounds, Bobby and I took off our mittens and stood in broad streetlight, flipping the pages, oblivious to our surroundings. Lori and Robbie concentrated on figure eights; we concentrated on Hamil-Camel toes. We were getting stiff; cold weather really makes exposed fingers rigid and a motionless body numb.

Lori knew what we were up to, and it's not like we were trying to hide it anyway. She blurted, "I'm telling your parents you're looking at dirty magazines."

She said it only to me, not Bobby. Great, now I'm in trouble. I'd have to answer to my father (although he probably really wouldn't care) and to Father at confession.

Time to think fast. Maybe I could threaten her with telling her parents about the dirty record she had. Lori had a 45-rpm record of Terry Jacks' 1974 hit *Seasons in the Sun*. The "B" side was a song called *Put the Bone In*. It wasn't a really a "dirty" song; it was about a woman at a butcher shop pleading with the butcher to throw the bone in with her meat because her dog was hit by a car and she wanted to bring him something to make him feel better. The song ended with "Put the bone in, she begged him once more." On second thought.

I couldn't use that ditty for blackmail because we got a good laugh out of it. It wouldn't have been a good tit for tattle. My mind raced to figure a way out of this jam. I had to make Lori think I really wasn't looking at a *Playboy*, but some other magazine. No, not *Penthouse*, but a family friendly one, like *Boys' Life*. We usually had one laying around the house. Oh sure, what boy doesn't read that magazine under a streetlight on a cold winter night? ("Look at this ad. It says I can make money selling packages of seeds!"). Hey, it's all I had.

The first phase of my stage act was slinking away from the

rink unnoticed, so to the *Pink Panther* theme song I slipped away and walked kitty-corner to our house. I left my winter gear and skates on when I wandered about the house looking for *Boys' Life*. Surprisingly, no one asked me what the hell I was doing. They must have been catatonic, under the influence of television radiation. I finally found the magazine and went outside for Act II.

I couldn't just walk back to the rink and show Lori the magazine. I had to magically materialize like I had never left and show her she was mistaken about our reading material. In stage illusion, it's called the "prestige." This was getting as complicated as a Siegfried and Roy magic act; I needed to trade the pink panther for a white tiger. I wonder if something like my predicament every happened in Roy's life?

To make this work, I had to reappear from the snow bank along the north end of the rink. I had my work cut out for me; I would have to emerge from the north side of the stadium to get to that snow bank unnoticed. This meant backtracking all the way around the stadium, more than a quarter-mile, wearing skates.

With no other choice, I headed west on Hughitt Street, away from the rink, running on my tippy-toes, the fastest way to move on pavement wearing skates. I turned right on Birch Street at the Vondale's house. Rosie wasn't outside sweeping the driveway this night, so she couldn't help. I didn't need a chair prop anyway. I skate-walked north along the west stadium wall and then turned east on the back road behind the stadium. The last, long stretch lay ahead, a little over one hundred yards.

I peeked around the northeast corner of the stadium and saw the three of them were still there. I hoped they hadn't noticed I was gone. A lot of open ground lay between me and the snow bank along the edge of the rink. Lucky for me, I'd watched the *Sands of Iwo Jima* and *Back to Bataan* several times and knew what to do. Thank God, I didn't need any inspiration from *The Dirty Dozen;* I didn't have any hand grenades to toss down a roof vent. I crouched down and ran to the snow bank, hit the deck, cradled the *Boys' Life* in my arms like a rifle, and belly-crawled behind the bank. When the coast was clear, I popped up and casually walked to the light pole and tossed the magazine ahead of me. When I got to the light, I picked it up and shouted to Lori, "See, we were reading a *Boys' Life.*" A lot of work went into that.

"No you weren't," she said, "I saw you come from over there and throw the magazine."

Great, all that for nothing. When four people are skating and twenty-five percent of them suddenly disappear, I guess it's too much to expect that no one would notice. Maybe, I should have let Bobby in on my scheme and left him behind as an *agent provocateur.* I gave up, left my magazines, and went home to let the fickle finger of fate do what it might.

This time when I got home, I took off my skates. I was sitting at the kitchen table when someone knocked on the door. It was Lori serving her warrant. One of my brothers answered the door, and I could see Lori and Robbie standing in our little covered porch. Lori had a smirk on her face; she knew she had me. My brother told Mom someone was at the door to see her (great, another free turkey).

Mom went to the door and Lori said, "Mrs. Flaminio, Tom was looking at a dirty magazine at the ice rink."

I guess I'm in trouble now.

"OK, thanks," Mom said politely and shut the door.

That's it? I was off the hook, but now I wanted revenge. I was hoping Mom would shatter the glass case marked "In Case of Vonns Break Glass," grab the wooden spoon, and chase Lori down Hughitt Street as she had her brother.

The Russians Are Coming!

Every four years or so, Mom's family, the Hazuses, would visit, like a condensed cicada moth cycle. They'd always drive to Iron Mountain— either Grandma or Grandpa with Mom's brothers and sisters. Grandma and Grandpa never visited us together because they didn't live together. Grandma lived in Pennsylvania, and Grandpa lived in England, where he retired after his U.S. Air Force civilian career. Grandpa would fly to Pennsylvania and then drive to Iron Mountain with his kids. They had a "non-traditional marriage." Most people believe marriage should be practiced in the same house. Grandma and Grandpa believed marriage should be practiced in the same hemisphere.

Grandpa Hazus was a big Lithuanian-Ukrainian who looked like Joseph Stalin. He had the same thick head of salt and pepper hair, and a bushy moustache; he weighed close to 300 pounds and had a big, booming voice. The similarities stopped at genocide. He'd tell us stories of how he'd picked tomatoes for ten cents an hour as a young man. "But my picking days are over," he'd say contentedly. Grandpa got ten cents more an hour than Robert got for tomato picking.

One of my enduring memories of Grandpa was his sitting at the kitchen table, eating half a cantaloupe, an "exotic" fruit in our house. He was content as hell with his half-melon, spooning out the pulp and slurping it down. He looked so happy I almost felt like putting a cereal box in front of him to read. For some reason, milk was Grandpa's nemesis. One time at our house, he was lecturing someone about how milk wasn't good for you. I guess you could say he was lactose intolerant. He ended his lecture by telling his son, "Richard, pour me a glass of milk." It's a good thing that by then we had canceled our home milk delivery. That poor milkman would have been no match for the Russian bear. During another of his visits, Grandma and Grandpa Flaminio came over. When everyone was in the living room shooting the breeze about insignificant topics and politics, Grandpa Hazus steered the conversation to milk. I could imagine him saying, "Jimmy Carter, hell. Milk, now there's a problem in this country!"

It wasn't my imagination though when he said to my other grandfather, "Hell, Art, if you were meant to drink milk, you'd still be sucking on your mother's tit." Crickets chirped in the silence. I don't remember there being a request for a show of hands, but I'm sure no one in the room wanted to imagine Grandpa Flaminio suckling at his mother's teat.

When Grandma Hazus visited, she always drove a Cadillac. I remember in order a gold, a sky blue, and a brown Caddy. The gold and sky blue Cadillacs were early 1970s Fleetwoods; we thought they looked like the Batmobile. The brown one was a later 1970s model when they moved away from the iconic design. Cornelius Alesandrini had the only other Cadillac in town that I remember. Cornelius's nickname was "Torpedo," and he was the head of the laborer's union in Iron Mountain. His Cadillac was a convertible, one of the 1975 limited edition Bombay Yellow El Dorados. That thing was a boat; the Flaminio kids' in their funkadelic clothing would have been right at home aboard Torpedo's yellow submarine.

Any neighbor who saw Grandma's Cadillac's parked in front of our house would know the Flaminios had family in town. Let's see, a Cadillac parked in front of an old, weathered house full of kids and a yard strewn with bikes and toys; no stereotype there.

Once Grandma Hazus came to town, stayed for a day or two, and then flew to Las Vegas for a mini-vacation (Hi Grandma. Where are you going?). When she came back, she brought some presents. One was a miniature dime slot machine, a one-armed bandit. One-armed? Did someone beat us to breaking it? Well, at least it would look right at home on the shelf next to Mom's Hummels.

We loved driving around town in Grandma's Cadillac to see what the peasants were up to. Once Mom's sister Debbie took some of us for a luxury cruise. Debbie was in her early twenties and Grandpa's godson Boris, who came this Hazus visit, was a teen-ager. We wound up at the pit on Pine Mountain. It was a caved-in mine surrounded by rock cliffs with an ice-cold, blue-green pool of water; a lot of kids jumped off the cliffs and swam there. A flat area at the west end of the pool was covered with shale, those flat, flaky rocks that were good for skipping across the water. We held a skipping contest at the water's edge, and after the rock cliffs echoed with Carter's victory cry, "I couldn't sleep at all last night!," we sat on a big pile of shale fragments to hunt for fossils. We grabbed rocks left and right, looking for prehistoric creepy crawler impressions.

After coming up empty-handed, I had a brainstorm. Normally, it takes millions of years for fossilization (or thousands depending on your worldview), so why not speed up the process. I figured I could time warp a fossil and place it on the bait pile. Debbie and Boris came all the way from Pennsylvania, and I couldn't have them go home empty-handed. My fossil hoax was ingenious; who would fall for my rock bluff?

What to create? I could keep it simple and make a fish skeleton or a bug. No, I was going all in, I'd scratch Paleolithic cave art like in the Lascaux caves in France. They didn't seem to require too much artistic talent anyway. In the back of a *Boys' Life*, I never saw one of those "Draw Spunky the Skunk and Win $5,000" commercial art school contests based on a caveman horse drawing. Everyone was so engrossed in fossil hunting that no one noticed me scratching away at a rock, except Carter. I think he was burning ants by directing sunlight through his glasses. I used the sharp tip of a rock to scratch onto another a running stick figure man holding a spear over his head chasing an Ice Age buffalo. While everyone was distracted, I inconspicuously placed the "fossil" in the rock pile. Within a few minutes, Boris exclaimed "Look at this!" Hook—line— sinker. He bit that rock fish hard. As he proudly showed us his cave man Picasso and envisioned his world tour sponsored by the Smithsonian Institution, I couldn't hold it in any more and burst out laughing.

~~~

Our front porch was elevated off the ground by concrete blocks at each corner, so if we crouched down you could fit underneath. One afternoon, I saw Boris go around the side of the porch and duck under it. He didn't see me, so I peeked and saw him hunched and kneeling with a cigarette in his mouth, striking a match. He was a teenager, so he probably shouldn't have been smoking. But then again maybe Grandpa Hazus wouldn't care as long as he wasn't drinking milk. I stepped away, kept my mouth shut, and let him enjoy his smoke. Just then, Carter strolled out the porch and down the steps. Boris heard him, made a hasty retreat from under the porch and walked out to the front. Carter saw him coming from the side of the porch and knew what he was up to.

"What were you doing under there?" Carter said in a gotcha' tone. "Taking a pee?"

Poor Boris, bad enough he was burned with a fake fossil, now he was caught "relieving himself." Urine trouble now. He just pointed his finger at Carter, smiled and said, "Riiiigghhtt." Nice try, Boris, but I knew the truth, and it was Kool.

Hey, Goombadi (She Was So Naughty)

Soon after we moved to Iron Mountain, Steve and I were casing the neighborhood and wound up on the 1300 block of West "A" Street. We were strolling down the side walk when we heard, "Hey, kid." It was Bobby Doney, who would become my best childhood friend. He was inside his enclosed porch, talking to us through the screen window. I don't think that's how the priest talked to me through the screen at my first confession.

Bobby was my age, and his sister Debbie was ten years older. Debbie was a good-looking girl, which was obvious by all the boys who would show up at their house. His brother Mike was eight years older than us. I guess he wasn't too bad-looking either. Bobby's mom, Lucy, worked at the Dickinson Inn, which housed the Kentucky Fried Chicken. Debbie worked for Colonel Sanders, so we had someone on the inside for bucket rides.

Bobby's dad, also named Bob, was a pleasant, easy-going man with one of those mellow radio voices. He could have been in a 1950s television sitcom. I never saw him angry, except one time. Bobby and I had this brilliant plan to pulverize chunks of concrete, make powdered concrete, add water to make it soupy concrete, and then let it harden. Ah yes, the old Carnation brand liquid milk to powdered milk back to liquid milk shape-shifting trick. We just needed something to pound the concrete with. Bobby went into the house, came back out and said, "What about these," as he showed me some of his dad's golf clubs. Perfect! They even had grips on them, so we could really swing away. We placed the concrete chunks on the sidewalk and started pounding away. Bobby told me to keep my head down and tuck in my right elbow. His dad came home from work and found us wallowing in our twisted logic. Needless to say, he wasn't too happy. I remember him picking up one of the clubs by the handle, lifting the other end up to his face and gasping "My new driver!" He told me to go home, and who could blame him? Walking home, I reflected on the valuable lesson I had learned from this unfortunate incident; irons break up concrete a lot better than woods.

Mr. Doney was a radio operator on a bomber during World War II, flying in the European Theater. He was awarded the Distinguished Flying Cross, among other medals, at the ripe young age of 21. Anyone who'd flown on a bomber while German cannons were trying to make Swiss Cheese out of his B-24 could have been excused for being on edge, but he was always calm. I was impressed that he was in the Army Air Corps during the war because I loved watching World War II movies on TV.

Every week I'd pore through the *TV Guide* looking for a war movie. Back then, the *TV Guide* was a small booklet like the *Readers Digest.* Today, it's a full size magazine you curl up with at night or a station you find channel surfing. *TV Guide* was the most read magazine in America, and we contributed our fair share to that statistic. This was surprising, as the reading didn't involve breakfast packaging. Every week, at least the weeks Kathy didn't beat me to it, I attempted the crossword puzzle in the back of the magazine. Granted, it wasn't *The New York Times* crossword puzzle, but I did learn that Ra is an Egyptian Sun God and Rae is a Charlotte actress.

Mom would pick a *TV Guide* up while grocery shopping every

week, and when she came home, there'd be a treasure hunt. Several of us would rush the kitchen table, overflowing with grocery bags, not to help Mom put away the goods, but to find the oracle that would divine which shows would receive our open-mouthed gazes the following week.

When I found it, the first thing I did was zip through the program listings looking for any phrase or word with a hint of a war movie like "John Wayne" or "battle" or "Japanese on Gilligan's Island." I especially liked the *World at War* series narrated by Laurence Olivier; I never missed it.

Mr. Doney told me his squadron flew from their base in England, bombed German cities and then continued east to Russian-occupied territory. There they'd land, refuel, and head back to England. I was very impressed. I wondered if any of the damage Mom had seen in Frankfurt was from his bombing runs. The Doneys had a framed picture of a young, raven-haired Mr. Doney wearing his leather flight jacket and cap, oozing that flyer swagger. Mr. Doney had my dad's war wounds beat.

Bobby's grandpa, Matt Doney, lived next door to them. He had fought in World War I and Bobby had his steel doughboy helmet and gas mask. One day Bobby said, "My grandpa fought in World War I, and my dad fought in World War II, can you top that?" He had me there. I could have bluffed with Dad's Viet Cong bullet scars, but he would have seen right through that blemished story. He was holding aces; I had nothing. Later at home I told Mom of Bobby's hand. She said, "Well, just tell him you come from a family with ten kids and four sets of twins, can you top that?" I folded.

Bobby had a small record player that played 33-, 45- and 78-rpm records. We always played his 45-rpm Johnny Cash record, "A Boy Named Sue." I couldn't understand why a man would name his son Sue. You know damn well that on Christmas morning that guy told Susie to his face that the freakin' Lionel train was the old man's.

The other 45 we always played was that catchy Lou Monte Italian sing-along, "Hey Goombadi." The lyrics started out *"Hey Goombadi, ci vo suonare...."* To me, the lyrics began with, "Hey Goombadi, she was so naughty," and then I had no idea what they were singing. Even though we couldn't make out the lyrics, we loved it. It's a catchy tune; check it out on the Internet.

~~~

Locals tossed their household junk in a neighborhood dump. We liked to rummage through it; hoping one man's trash was another man's Mrs. Trembath-certified treasure. Bobby and I were picking through the dump once and found an album that we judged by its colorful cover. We didn't know it was a Rodgers and Hammerstein musical, but that *Carousel* album looked cool. We thought we'd hit the jackpot (but not the World War II era Broadway show *Jackpot*, which bombed). Who would throw a perfectly good album in the dump? We had to play it right away, so we jumped on our bikes and raced to Bobby's house.

Bobby's brother Mike was in the living room, where Bobby kept his record player. But that was OK; we didn't care if his teen age brother listened to *Carousel* too. We turned on the player, moved the lever from the *Hey Goombadi* 45-rpm to the *Carousel* 33-rpm, dropped the needle and anticipated, like waiting for ketchup to hit our burgers. A few notes into the first song, we glanced at each other, a little embarrassed. Wow, this kind of music. We pretended we liked it, but Broadway musicals weren't cool.

Mike, sitting on the couch next to us, couldn't take it anymore. "This is stupid. Why did you even bring this here?"

He was right; I bet the stocky boxer turned actor Tony Galento would never appear in a musical like *Carousel*. Bobby and I wanted to forget we'd ever brought this album to his house. It was a memory you push to the dark recesses of your mind, only to relive it when your life flashes before your eyes, or when someone writes about it forty years later. It made us both long for the comforting, incomprehensible lyrics of "*Hey Goombadi.*" Maybe there was a reason that album was in the dump.

I liked to go to the Doney's house on Friday or Saturday nights, their usual Brutomessos pizza nights. Takeout pizza was a luxury item in our family, so we exploited any chance to have pizza, especially from Brutomessos. They made pizza the way all the Iron Mountain pizza joints did and the way God intended — thin crust, cut in squares.

For us, pizza was usually Chef Boy-ar-Dee instant. It came in a box with all the packaged ingredients. Just add water to the little packet of dry mix to make the dough. No yeast, no setting, and no proofing the dough and letting it rise. We would spread the dough on an oiled pan, pour the little can of sauce over it, and sprinkle on the little packet of powdered cheese. That was it. We always made it in a big rectangular pan. Carter liked it best and was the designated *pizzaioli*. Come to think of it, they weren't that bad. At that time, frozen pizzas weren't nearly the quality they are today, unless you liked ketchup-covered cardboard. Too bad Mom wasn't able to make a half instant, half real pizza.

One Saturday morning, I was up early and decided to head over to Bobby's house. Maybe I wanted to score some Brutomesso's leftovers — don't mind me, finish your bacon and eggs; I'll just munch on this cold pizza and put on *Hey Goombadi.*

The neighborhood was quiet when I walked over to his house; it was late autumn with frost on the ground. When I approached Bobby's house, I saw some white, creamy piles next to the sidewalk. As I got closer, I saw it was Cool Whip, another rare treat. What a waste of good dessert topping, but at the same time, what a great opportunity! If there had been a blueberry patch nearby, I'd have been in heaven.

I looked around to see if anyone was watching, and, as far as I could tell, it was just Clarence Birdseye and me. I extended my mustard finger and dipped it in, pulling up a dollop of that creamy goodness.

Ugh. That had to be the bitterest whipped cream ever, with a taste that could grow hair on your face. This would have been appropriate because I had just eaten shaving cream. The Doney's had a hunting camp, and sometimes I'd go there with Bobby to spend the night. When we were around thirteen, his dad would let him drive their car around the camp. We'd drive up and down the gravel drive and loop around a tree in front of the camp. Their car had a CB radio, and we'd pretend we were *Starsky and Hutch*, calling the station and chasing bad guys. Bobby was Starsky, but I wasn't allowed to be Huggy Bear.

Starsky and Hutch was one of our favorite shows. Of course, the best episode was "Murder on Playboy Island," a two-part, two-hour event. A television cop drama and centerfolds, two great tastes that taste great together. The plot involved mysterious murders at a swinger's hotel on a secluded tropical island. The best part was that one of the actresses took her role to heart, and, like all thespians devoted to their craft, immersed herself in her character's real world. Centerfold Patti McGuire played the role of Pussycat. Meow.

Root Beer, Pig Brain, and Water Buffalo

The Ellingson brothers, Mark and Mike, lived next door to Angie Godin. Mark was a few years older than Mike; both graduated high school in the early '70s. They were more like big brothers to us, the kind that didn't have to fill out paperwork. Like the Rahois next door to us, they went above and beyond being good neighbors, and we were lucky to have them.

The Ellingsons always had Oreo cookies in their house, which was reason enough for us to go over there. If any grapes were out of reach when we walked by Angie's gazebo, we'd satisfy our sweet tooth with their cookies. We rarely had Oreos in our house because they were more expensive than the generic equivalents from the Red Owl, or that brand called Hydrox. I never knew why they named a cookie after a chemical.

Mike and Mark would load as many of us that would fit in their cars and take us joyriding. The biggest treat was when they took us to one of two root beer joints, A&W or Dog'n Suds. We used to drop subtle hints that we wouldn't mind stopping for a root beer; as we passed one, someone would say, "Uh oh, there goes A&W."

One day Mark took Jim, John, Moomer, and Tony for a ride in his truck, which back then meant riding in the truck bed. That was always fun, feeling wind blowing your hair. If you drive four grade-schoolers around in a truck bed today, you would be plastered all over TV on a BREAKING NEWS update from a helicopter. John was sitting close to the edge of the truck bed and fell out. As Mark was driving away, Jim, Tony, and Moomer pounded frantically on the window of the cab, yelling, "Mark! Mark! Mark!" It took awhile for Mark to respond (Man, those Flaminios are getting aggressive with their root beer requests.) When he finally turned around and saw their panic, it was no problem; he just went back, threw John back in, and continued driving. A trip to Dog 'n Suds would buy their silence.

One afternoon Mike, Mark and their friends rolled a huge, inflatable black rubber pillow around their yard, it was about eight feet long and four feet high. Their dad had brought it home from his railroad job. I could only imagine what titanic head laid on it at night hearing The Wolfman's coal shoveling in the pillow's air-filled void. One of them said "Let's roll this over the Flaminios!" and before we knew it, we were laying on the ground being steamrolled by the gargantuan pillow. Getting stepped on was an even trade for a good time.

The Ellingson brothers gave us a pig brain in a glass baby food jar. Maybe it really was infant food from France. *Jerbert* brand, *oui*? I had heard they eat every part of the animal over there. Mom's jars of pigs' feet in our refrigerator were a testament to European eating habits. I remember the brain had bright, colorful, cobalt blue veins. I could imagine them doing some house cleaning one day, deciding whether to toss it and saying, "Let's give it to the Flaminios." The brain was preserved in a formaldehyde bath and the lid was sealed a lot better than a pickle jar. I wondered if the pig who gave his brain to science was related to the maimed pigs who donated their parts to Mom's jars. A few of us took turns "owning" the brain and displaying it in our bedrooms.

The Ellingsons had a Ouija board on their porch, this was the "spirit board" popular in the 1970s for séances. It was a flat board with the alphabet, numbers, and the words "Yes" and "No" printed on it. A small, heart-shaped piece of wood, called a planchette, had a circular window in the middle. Two people each put their fingertips on one side of the planchette and asked a question out loud to the otherworldly entity. When the "spirit" answered, the planchette would move and stop with the little window right over a letter, repeating until it spelled a word. I always wondered why a game based on spelling had a name that was spelled not even close to how it was pronounced (Wee-jee is how we all said it.) What if a spirit was bad at spelling or was dyslexic? Would his bad spelling channel through the participants? Or would the board censor his spelling and correct it? And what about the converse? What if the spirit was Einstein and one of the participants was an idiot? Would something get lost in the translation? When teenagers play Ouija, does the "spirit" answer in texting language — CUL8R?

Robert and I gave it a whirl, knowing full well it wasn't a Vatican-approved recreation. Robert's vision was so bad we should have used a Braille Ouija. At first we asked it mundane questions to feel it out. Just like a quiz in school, the first questions are no-brainers (like a certain pig). Sure enough, the planchette moved across the board, stopping on letters, spelling words. I can't remember what they were; all I do remember is how stunned we were. We both looked at each other in amazement.

"I'm not moving it. Are you moving it?" I said.

"No, I'm not moving it," Robert said.

We were scared and intrigued at the same time. At one point we asked Ouija if Tony Sacchetti would break his leg skiing in the coming winter. I have no idea why we were concerned with Satch's leg bones. Maybe I should have asked about my blue skis. This little exercise proved how ridiculous the Ouija board was. He didn't break his leg skiing that winter. He broke it sledding.

They had a Rockem' Sockem' Robot game on the porch too, two plastic robots on a platform, boxing each other. One robot was blue and one red, a precursor to the modern day political divide in America. The players controlled the robots' punches with two joysticks, one for each arm. They could only throw right and left uppercuts, no jabs or roundhouses because, after all, they were robots. A round ended when one of the robot's spring-loaded heads popped up from a good punch. We could tell that one of the robots had a glass jaw because his head would pop up from even the weakest punch. His jaw broke easier than Satch's leg.

They also stashed *Playboys* under the front porch with the Ouija Board. I always thought they "forgot" to lock the porch on purpose for us. Maybe we could have run the planchette over a centerfold to see what happened. There was a couch on the porch, and if someone walked by the house, they would see some Flaminio boys sitting on it, sizing up the centerfold. That would have been an interesting conversation if the mailman had walked up to the porch:

"Hi boys."

"Hi Mr. Jackson. Say Hi to Dad when you get back at the Post Office."

"Sure thing. You know, I think he has that issue."

There was an apple tree in the Ellingsons' front yard, and we liked those apples just like our grapes — green and sour. Like Angie, the Ellingsons suffered crop loss every year, although we never heard a disembodied voice from their house telling us to stay away. Tomatoes, apples, and grapes, we picked them all from our neighbors, and we did it for free. We never got a cease and desist order from the United Farm Workers.

We'd tuck in our t-shirts and load green apples down our shirts until we had a potbelly. We'd ride our bikes all over the neighborhood, reach into the pouch and grab an apple, eat it, and then toss the core in the nearest yard, regenerating a renewable resource. Dad wasn't the only Flaminio male good at planting seeds.

One summer Jim, John, and Tony used the stop sign on Angie's corner for green apple target practice. Eventually, the city replaced the sign. I imagine it was routine maintenance and had nothing to do with the applesauce, apple cider, apple juice and apple turnover caking the sign.

One summer evening, Mike Ellingson and a posse of other older boys were chasing a rat around the neighborhood. A real one, not a Mafia snitch. Some of my brothers and I cheered them on. They corralled it into a basement window well at the end of the block. Between Mike and his BB gun and another kid with his bow and arrow, that rat was toast. We marched down the alley with the carcass on a slab of wood, right by Grandpa Jack's garage, not at all shamed by the otter and beaver pelts inside that labeled us amateurs. When we reached Mike's house, the older boys decided to have a rat fry in the back yard burn barrel. Mike's mom asked Mike what he had.

"It's a rat," said Mike.

She looked at it, and in a disappointed voice, she said, "Aw Mike, it's a woodchuck."

Barbequed woodchuck, would have been nice with Angie's grapes and the Ellingsons' apples around it for presentation.

The Ellingsons had a hunting dog, a bluetick named Chip for his spots that looked like potato chips. Chippy stayed in a in a big pen next to the alley, and when we walked by, he'd run up to greet us. It's too bad Chippy hadn't taught our dog Spanky proper manners. Chippy had a lot of pent up energy, and when he was out of the pen, he'd zoom all over the place.

When John was four or five, Chippy was out of his pen and bolted after John. A horrified John took off like a Laotian sprinter. He ran through Angie's yard, racing for Maple Street and then asylum at our house. When Chippy caught him at Angie's, John's scream pierced the neighborhood. When we looked over at the sound of John's terror and watched him get tackled by a dog as big as he was, we all thought the same thing, "Hey, Angie's grapes are green enough to eat."

The Ellingsons' gave us a big, green, canvas Army tent, just like one on the TV show *M*A*S*H*. A playhouse from one neighbor, an army tent from the Ellingsons', at this rate we thought we would get a pop-up camper from a neighbor someday. Mosquitoes were squatting in the foreclosed Mosca playhouse, so we thought we'd have better luck with recreational lodging from a different neighbor. Even though the tent didn't have a floor, we still used it for some rugged camping in our back yard.

On one warm summer night, Carter, Robert, and I were ready for a malaria-free night under the stars. As we settled in, we heard "thunk, thunk, thunk" against the canvas. Dang those mosquitoes are getting big. I went outside and saw green apples lying on the ground. Steve and his friends were down the alley bombarding us. We cabled the honorably discharged U.S. Air Force Sergeant in our house who called an on the spot, non-negotiable cease-fire. We had a midnight snack of green apples and called it a night.

The Ellingsons' also gave us a water buffalo horn. Pig brain, water buffalo horn, what the hell was going on over there? The horn was loud and sounded like a trombone. Maybe during the communion ceremony at Mass, the priest would let me answer "The Body of Christ" with that horn. Sometimes, we'd go outside, stand on the front steps, blow the horn, and then go back inside the house, reminding the neighbors, "Yeah, we're still here."

One winter afternoon, Tony came home and said Rick Gingras, the Ellingsons' next-door neighbor, had thrown a snowball at him. Sure, it was just a playful toss, but truth is the first casualty of war. The Band of Brothers mobilized and donned winter gear for the enemy encounter. No worries about cold feet, we had real, bread bag-free boots by then.

It was as if one of us had blown that buffalo horn, and the brothers parachuted into the neighborhood, or at least umbrella-jumped off the back roof. Poor Rick didn't know what hit him. It was a classic pincer attack, a right flank and left flank assault. We left his carcass in his driveway; the wounded enemy wasn't our problem.

Road Trip!

Since 1976 was an election and Olympic year, the odds were good Mom's family would visit us in Iron Mountain. However, in the true Spirit of '76, we broke the manacles of royal tradition and took our one and only family vacation to Pennsylvania to visit the Hazus clan. We drove to Wilkes-Barre, in the Pocono Mountains located at the east end of the state. Mom and Dad must have really pinched hard to save money for the trip. Fed us instant milk instead of half-and-half? Tore the back page of the Christmas catalogue? Somehow, they managed.

Before we left, we had to find a sucker, ah neighbor, to look after our dog, the demon spawn Spanky. Mark Ellingson drew the short straw. The morning we left, we brought Spanky over to Mark's, chained him to the clothesline post and left Mark some dog food (now he's your problem). Sorry about that Mark.

We hit the road with the Travelall pulling a U-Haul trailer. Mom and Dad were in the front with one of either Jim, John, Moomer or Tony, four kids were on the middle bench seat, and the last five in the back cargo area. Everything was right with that setup, the AAA-approved 3-4-5 family road-trip configuration. This seating arrangement must have been legal because the cops never pulled us over. We looked — a bunch of people with long, moppy 1970s hair — a lot like a traveling summer stock production of *Jesus Christ Superstar.* I guess we were the twelve apostles. I rode in the back cargo space for most of the trip. I liked it back there because there were pillows and I could sprawl out, as much as possible with four other kids. I also had my stack of magazines to enjoy. *MAD*, not *Playboy*. Air conditioning ate up fuel and hauling all these people and a trailer strained the engine, so Dad used the cold air sparingly, if at all. We were twelve bodies in a hot, confined space; good thing we were family. All that was missing was a T.V. and a fan.

I spent a little time on the bench seat. It got uncomfortable, especially when I tried napping. However, it didn't take us long to discover the perfect resting position. We'd kneel on the floor facing the seat with our arms folded, one over the other, and lay our head on our arms. We looked like we invented a hybrid *tai chi* position, the "kneel at church/put your head down on your desk for misbehaving in class." It was comfortable and a good way to catch some shuteye, hypnotized by the drone of the tires vibrating through the seat.

During the trip, all we could think about was Grandma's swimming pool. Cadillacs and a heated swimming pool in the Poconos — we're going high society! According to family legend, Mom's grandmother, who had lived next door to Grandma Hazus, had buried money in the yard. If this is like looking for money in the stadium, it's going to be a piece of cake (not my sister Kathy's). Plus, now we had a metal detector. Maybe Mom hadn't torn that back page off the Christmas catalogue after all.

We stopped now and then for bathroom breaks or rest stop lunches, climbing out of the Travelall like a never-ending line of circus clowns. Speaking of clowns, maybe nobody can do it like Ronald McDonald can, but fast-food stops were few and far between on this trip. I think we stopped one time at a fast food joint. We stored bologna sandwiches and moist cake and cookies Mom had baked before the trip in the metal trailer, our rations baking in the reflective heat from the interstate asphalt. After wolfing down our rest stop lunches, we'd pile in the Travelall, and Mom would do a head count. Then she'd count again and recount until she finally declared there were twelve electoral votes in the car.

We made it to Toledo on the first day. Not bad from Iron Mountain. That's about five hundred miles, fifty miles per kid. Driving though Ohio, we stopped on the turnpike a few times to pay tolls. I never knew you had to give money to a guy in a ticket booth to drive on a highway; maybe we could sneak by this guy too.

From Ohio, we entered Pennsylvania, but we still had to cross the state. We finally made it over the river and through the hills to Grandma Hazus' house after two full days of driving. We pulled into the driveway and disembarked. I swear, a few of us didn't even exchange pleasantries. We ran right around the house to the front yard to check out the pool. Oh, it's one of those big above-ground pools. Well, that's better than no pool. We went for a closer look, ready to plunge in our arms for a warm water bath. As we got closer, we saw leaves and other floaties in the pool. We dipped our hands in, and the water didn't feel warm at all. And what's that green stuff in the pool? Is that algae? Oh well, at least John has something to drink.

We soon found out the Hazuses had a German shepherd named Chelsea. They hadn't told us about that. Dad didn't like that dog. Whenever the pooch was in the house, Dad told someone to put her outside. I don't know why Dad didn't like her, she only looked like Condor.

Our Philadelphia relatives, Uncle Angelo Troisi and his daughter Andrea, our cousin, were there when we arrived. Angelo was married to Grandpa Hazus' sister, Leona, who had passed away a few years earlier at a Frank Sinatra concert at the Spectrum in Philadelphia. If you're going to heaven, I can't think of a better send-off than Old Blue Eyes crooning *Somebody To Watch Over Me*.

Angelo was a typical short Italian guy with a great sense of humor. He's also very generous. When Mom and Dad and their three infants left the Air Force base in England for Dad's next station in New Jersey, there was no base housing available, and we had nowhere to stay. Angelo took us in, putting the five of us in a room in his West Philly townhouse. Even though there was Angelo's family and his mother-in-law (my great-grandmother), he saw to it that we had a warm bed to sleep in. My parents said they don't know what they would have done if not for Uncle Angelo. For about a month, Dad took the bus everyday to McGuire Air Force Base until he found a house to rent.

Like us, Angelo must have had exaggerated visions of Grandma's pool because he was ready for some poolside sun bathing. He came out of the house wearing his bathing suit, or what apparently passed as a bathing suit in Philadelphia; he was wearing boxer shorts. Perhaps, that's how he cooled off at open fire hydrants during big city heat waves like I'd see on TV.

Uncle Angelo spread his towel on the ground next to the pool, ready to add a bronze hue to his copper tone. He must have wanted to radiate his crown too because he tore off his toupee. It looked like he was pulling off one of Grandpa Jack's muskrat pelts.

Angelo looked a lot better with his rug than the crazy guy Dad had chased from our porch a few years earlier. After Angelo scalped himself, I found out that hair pieces stick to bald heads with tape. I guess it's one of those things I had never thought about. At least if Carter and Robert broke their glasses, they wouldn't have far to go for a repair kit.

Andrea had just completed her first year of college and told us she was studying art therapy, the craft which people draw pictures and the therapist looks for clues in the art to the person's troubles. We took turns drawing pictures, so she could analyze them using her vast reservoir of freshman wisdom. I drew a house and a tree with a trunk that fanned out at the bottom. She told me a trunk drawn that way meant something, but I can't remember what it was. I think it was "You have an uncanny ability to remember trivial events."

Later, I told Mom about Andrea studying to be an art therapist. She insisted I didn't hear her right. "No, she's going to be a heart therapist," Mom said.

"No," I said, "She's an art therapist."

"That can't be right," said Mom, "She's a heart therapist."

Whatever you say, Mom. I'll draw another picture for Andrea so she can tell me if I have cardiomyopathy

There was a pickle jar in the refrigerator, and lucky for Grandma, it was a regular size jar without the hand-size opening, what we called a "child resistant top." That was OK, because Grandma had a stash of Milky Way bars in the refrigerator, just like in the church rectory back home. But I wasn't in a church now.

At work, rest, and play, I made a good dent in Grandma's chocolate lode. After I decimated the stock, I tried to reconfigure the last few to create a horn of plenty illusion. No luck. I really needed a "seven loaves of bread and one fish miracle." One of my siblings committed the *coup de grace* and emptied the horn. I was the setup man; I don't know who the closer was.

Grandma didn't notice until it was too late, "Where are my Snickers?" she pleaded. "Who ate all my Snickers?"

Grandma thought they were Snickers. I know for a fact they were Milky Ways; their wrappers are a dead giveaway. Besides, every kid knows that chocolate malt nougat topped with caramel and covered with milk chocolate is a Milky Way. I can't believe Grandma confused it with peanut nougat topped with roasted peanuts and caramel and covered in milk chocolate.

I didn't know what the big deal was. Adults can buy candy bars any time they want. Mom chimed in too, "Someone ate all of Grandma's Snickers!" I knew legally I was in the clear. Go ahead, put me under a hot light and ask me who ate your Snickers; I have no idea. Your Milky Way bars, I know exactly where those went, but Snickers, sorry; I can't help you there Grams. I was waiting for her to sit us all down and make us draw pictures, so Andrea could analyze them to smoke out the perp.

We did a lot fun stuff the few days we were there. Debbie took us for a Cadillac ride to the Hickory Run Boulder Field, sixteen acres of boulders created during the last Ice Age. Because it was prehistoric geology, there was one thing on my mind: faux fossils. I had already checked Grandpa's godson off my fossil scam to-do list, but Debbie's name was still unmarked. However, looking at the size of those rocks, I realized I didn't have the time or proper tools for another Cro-Magnon hoax. A terra-cotta Chinese soldier from the Ming Dynasty would have looked cool though.

Uncle Rick took us fishing, which for us meant casting from shore and catching nothing. After we drowned all our worms, we went beer can hunting in the woods. Like a lot of kids, Carter and Robert were beer can collectors, especially of exotic brands not sold in Iron Mountain like Rolling Rock or Bartels. The woods were good for beer can scavenging because teenagers always had beer parties there.

Grandma Hazus owned a bar in town called The Swan. If Robert wanted beer cans, he should have just dug through the Swan's garbage cans.

One afternoon, we had a big party there for all the extended family. Mom made spaghetti (and it wasn't even the proper day of the week) and chili. Robert couldn't finish his chili, so he dumped it into what he thought was the chili pot but was actually the spaghetti sauce. Hey, just like they do in restaurants. No big deal, just another version of half-and-half.

Some of the Hazus clan and friends came down from Long Island, New York. For a lot of East Coasters, a family gathering is a good reason for a clambake. The New Yawkahs baked the clams in the half-shell with a spicy breadcrumb topping, giving them a crispy coating. Those crispy critters were quite a bit more elitist *frutti del mare* than the fish sticks with ketchup we had in landlocked Iron Mountain.

I feared for Carter, remembering from his Lake Antoine shell-picking expeditions, that Carter plus shellfish would equal a blind-side attack from Steve. Lucky for Carter, Steve's attack triggers were apparently fresh water species, not the oceanic varieties. As it turned out, it was a real nice clambake. Hey, the musical *Carousel* has a song, "It Was a Real Nice Clambake." At least, that's what someone told me.

We headed home after about four days. Four days of driving, four days of vacation, that's how we do it. When we turned onto Maple Street, we saw a chained Spanky sitting on our front step. He didn't look happy. It was like he was tapping his paw and saying, "Where the hell have you been?" He was supposed to be at the Ellingsons', but he got nippy, so Mark brought him back to our house and chained him at the doorstep where there was an overhanging roof to keep him shaded and dry.

Uncle Jerry and one of his friends had done Dad's janitor jobs while we were away, and they'd had trouble getting past Spanky to get in the house for the cleaning equipment. One of them had to keep him at bay with a stick while the other bolted into the house.

When we piled out of the Travelall and went to "greet" Spanky, he growled at us (yeah, he was ticked off) and didn't want anything to do with any of us, except Mom, of course. She was the only one allowed to pet him. The rest of us were on probation for a few days before he allowed us within biting distance.

Mikes, Bikes, and Pikes

The citizen band (CB) radio craze was full frenzy in the 1970s. It seemed everywhere you looked was a whip radio antenna on a car or a radio tower on a house roof. Everyone was getting CB radios; so naturally we got … walkie-talkies. At least the box they came in didn't say Fisher-Price. Our walkie-talkies could still communicate with CBs on channels 7 and 14, but most CB operators avoided those channels. They didn't want to associate with the low-frequency lifes.

The CBs could communicate thousands of miles when the radio waves skipped off the ionosphere, "shooting skip" as they called it. It was illegal in America, of course it was. The FCC wasn't going to bless long-distance communication without Ma Bell getting a cut of the action. Those lobbyists earned their paychecks.

Even though I didn't really understand the "skip" concept or the legal ramifications, I still liked to have fun with the idea. Using our "portable CB radio," I'd say in a southern accent something like, "Break skip line Northern Michigan, this is Southern Alabama. Come in." I'm sure I wasn't using proper CB lingo, and that certainly betrayed me to most radio operators, but a few of them took the bait and answered. I was all excited when that happened because it had actually worked, but then I always got flustered because I didn't know how to follow up, so I just turned it off.

One winter night, Carter, Robert and I were in the kitchen with one of the walkie-talkies and heard a crackling, faint girl's voice trying to make contact. "This is Giant Ice; come in, this is Giant Ice. This is Giant Ice, help me." What the heck, some girl called Giant Ice needed help. "This is Giant Ice; I'm stuck in a tree." Robert and I couldn't believe it; this girl was stuck in a tree. What fool climbs a tree on a cold, winter night? We were cracking up.

Carter tried to throw a bucket of cold reality on us. "That's Kathy," he said.

No it's not, it's Giant Ice. Maybe it sounds like Kathy and static, but it's Giant Ice and she's stuck in a tree. Shut up so we can hear what else this poor girl has to say.

"This is Giant Ice; hello, this is Giant Ice; I'm stuck in a tree," came the distant voice from the walkie talkie.

Our walkie-talkie had finally picked up a CB-worthy conversation! Robert and I looked at each other in amazement; Carter looked at us in disbelief.

Wait a minute, where's the other walkie-talkie?

When Kathy came out of the bathroom, laughing, she held the other walkie-talkie. Carter was right. He and his twin must have been on the same wavelength.

~~~

Our bike fleet was a hodgepodge of new bikes, rummage-sale bikes, hand-me-down bikes and bikes we might have "forgotten" to give back to friends. In the summer, between our bikes and our friends', there were so many of them lying in our yard, it looked like a Tour de France wipeout, without the performance enhancing drug allegations. These were the days, too, when no one wore bike helmets. The only helmets we were familiar with were football gear and my brother Tony's Dutch-boy haircuts.

In the 1970s, all kids had "banana bikes," the one-speed bikes with long seats shaped like a banana. They were more like saddles, perfect for riding double, and they were ideal for us because we didn't always have a one-to-one bike-to-kid ratio. We even rode triple on them, two on the seat and one on the handle bars. Today, you can only do the "triple threat" if you're monkeys in a circus act. What was once a good exercise in balance and coordination now gets you a lecture from a policeman.

A lot of our bikes weren't really owned by anyone; they were mostly on a first come, first served basis; it was a social bike ownership plan like 1950s Budapest. One was a gold girls' banana bike we got from the neighbors; or maybe it was a bike we used and never gave back. It didn't look like gold factory paint, it looked like it was a homemade job with a can of spray paint like the painted lady in *Goldfinger*. When Tony got excited, his voice would rise. When he screeched, "I get the golden bike!" you'd swear the little old lady across the street, Angie Godin, was calling dibs.

Robert and I played a game called "Where Am I?" on a banana bike. One of us sat on the handlebar with eyes closed, and the other rode the bike, making all kinds of twists, U-turns, and backtracks to confuse the contestant. After a while, he'd have to guess where he was. We honored the "Where Am I?" code of ethics and neither of us ever peeked. The game always seemed to end with the driver abruptly braking and trying to dump the rider on a lawn, driveway, alley; it didn't matter. There were no lovely parting gifts.

We had one bike where the pedals rotated when the bike was just pushed. One day Jim, John, and Tony made a life-sized dummy and tied its hands to the handle grips and the feet to the pedals. They laid in wait at the northeast corner of the stadium, and when a car came down Hughitt Street, they pushed the dummy-pedaling bike across the field. The mannequin made it about thirty yards or so before crashing. The driver of the car slammed on his brakes and came running out to help the poor kid who'd taken such a nasty spill. When he got to the bike and saw the dummy, he was mad as hell. He picked up the dummy-bike combo, slammed it on the on the ground, hopped back in his car, and took off.

Most adults had the larger, single-speed, single-seat bicycles—the cruisers. Some had a metal cage basket attached to the handlebars or two saddle baskets, one on each side of the rear tire. Kids with a handlebar cage basket on their banana bikes were looked at with sadness. Mom had a girl's blue cruiser, one of her rummage sale treasures. It was an old, been-through-the-wringer bike she affectionately called Old Blue. One afternoon, Mom and Moomer went to clean one of the offices for Dad's janitor business. Instead of driving though, they took Old Blue. Moomer sat on the handlebars holding a bucket of rags while Mom rode them down "A" Street. It was a tender, heart-warming mother-daughter moment they could share for a lifetime. All that was missing was their riding the bike in super-fast motion while being chased by that really old man and Benny Hill with his theme music.

~~~

We liked to fish (but not necessarily eat fish) when we were kids, though we really didn't know what we were doing. It was more about being outside and having fun than actually catching something. We liked to cast from shore and dream of catching a big fish, then we would wonder what we would do with it. We biked miles to either Lake Antoine or the Ford Dam on the Menominee River. That was common back then, kids pedaling their bikes and holding fishing poles.

One Saturday morning, we were fishing with Daredevil lures for northern pike on the Ford Dam backwater. I cocked the pole behind me and cast forward, but the lure snagged on something. It couldn't have been a trophy already. I heard Robert yell, "Ahhhhh." Oops. I hoped I'd hooked his Brillo pad-like hair.

I spun around and saw Robert with both his hands on the top of his head, the "under arrest" position, and through the prism of his thick plastic lenses, I could see he was crying. This was an emergency, time for an SOS. I grabbed some scissors from a tackle box and cut the line from the lure. The red and white Daredevil hooked in his head looked cool against his black, wiry hair. Today they just call it body piercing. Some guys wear baseball hats with fishing lures or hooks stuck in them. "Wimps," Robert calls them. Because Robert was in so much pain, Bobby Doney gave him a can of insect repellent and told him to squeeze it. Bobby must have thought that squeezing the can would alleviate the pain or maybe make Robert forget about it. Or maybe Bobby couldn't get any bug spray out of the can and wanted Robert to try to squeeze it out. We walked to the dam and told the attendant about the lure in Robert's head, thinking an adult would know what to do. "What am I supposed to do?" the man said. Oh well. I don't know, do you have a can of Lysol he could squeeze?

That dam guy at least let us use the phone, so we called home, and Mom showed up soon after. Getting a lure stuck in your head was more of an emergency than biting a radio tube or drinking swamp water. That was one of the few incidents in our family requiring a hospital visit. When Mom went to the hospital, she had to be on her toes for the orderlies' Pavlovian response to put her on a gurney and wheel her into a delivery room.

The emergency room doctor didn't use a squeeze can for pain management, he gave Robert a numb skull with a shot to his scalp and just yanked the lure out.

Another summer afternoon, we were fishing from the shore of Lake Antoine. Steve was using a juicy, purple rubber worm for bait. It looked like one of those Creepy Crawlers we made by pouring liquid into hot steel molds and letting them cool. His pole snapped down hard; he had a big one. As he reeled it in, we could see it was a huge largemouth bass. But it wasn't hooked as well as Robert's head had been, and close to shore, it got loose. The fish burrowed between some rocks in the shallows, and we could see the tailfin waving back and forth. Steve jumped in the water wearing his tennys, grabbed the fin and yanked it out. That sucker was a big bass.

We couldn't top that, so we called it a day. Now we had to find something to carry the fish in for the five-mile bike ride home. We found a bread bag (big surprise) and dropped it in. Since it was in a bread bag, that bass was at least a foot.

On the bike ride home, Steve proudly propped the trophy bass in his palm like a *maitre d* carrying a platter of cumin-crusted Chilean sea bass. Now Mom and Dad wouldn't have to go to the C&R Bar for fish fry. When we got home, we burst into the house to show them. They took one look at the dead fish and Dad said, "Nice. Get rid of it." Steve and I took the corpse outside, dug a hole in the back yard, dropped in the plastic-wrapped body and shoveled the dirt back on top under the approving eye of Vinny the Blowfish.

Brother, Can You Spare A Dime?

I was a paper boy art project on a Head Start wall and I was a paper boy for William Randolph Hearst's newspaper cronies. As our spending habits grew, Sunday morning stadium nickel-and-diming didn't cut it anymore and all of us boys lugged the *The Iron Mountain News*, *Milwaukee Journal* and *Green Bay Press Gazette* papers. If more people in town had read the *Green Bay Press Gazette* there wouldn't have been embarrassing questions to certain local guys about playing for the Packers.

In those days, we had to collect the money directly from the customers once a week. When I knocked on the door of one elderly Italian guy, Adriano Provenzano, he'd shuffle up and ask me how much he owed. I'd tell him, "Ninety cents."

He'd repeat it back to me, "Ninety cents"; then he'd just stare at me and breathe heavily. Maybe he was thinking back to the days when he was a young boy; I don't know, but he was intimidating. I didn't like collecting from him. Eventually, he stopped answering the door. I knew he wasn't hurt or worse because the newspapers weren't piling up on the porch. He was weeks behind on his payment, so I stopped delivering his paper. Thank God.

I thought I was done with Adriano for good, but Carter wouldn't let me forget him. Whenever we rode our bikes past his house,

Carter would yell, "Hey, Adriano, when you going to pay my brother?" I'd get all scared and pedal like hell out of there. I dreaded seeing Adriano one day shuffle out of the house and chase me just like then in a horror movie—lollygagging after me, yet somehow keeping right on my tail.

Mr. Balistieri, another old Italian guy on my route, also stared and breathed at me. Let me go on record that most of the old Italian guys in Iron Mountain were great. I guess a few of them didn't like paying for the paper. Every time I collected from Mr. Balistieri, he made me feel as if I were robbing him. *I know you lived through the Depression, but so did Angie Godin, and she lets us take her grapes.* When the weekly rate for newspaper delivery went up ten cents, I knew he wouldn't like it. I had two options— I could either tell him and have him breathing down my neck, or I could not tell him and eat that dime every week for the sake of peace. Grandpa Hazus picked tomatoes for ten cents an hour and I caved in for ten cents a week. That ten cents was still less painful than the canine Penny at the Landsee house.

It wasn't just cranky, old guys on my routes. There was a bald elderly lady on my paper route who covered her naked crown with a small black veil that resembled a teacup doily. It looked like she had leaves on her head, so we called her the "leave lady."

She was nice though, and a good tipper. Some women customers with full manes weren't as pleasant.

Once at Mrs. Mazilli's, I rang the bell, and when the door opened, she stared at me (normal breathing), and the first thing out of her mouth was "Jesus Christ Almighty, every time I turn around there's another goddamn paper boy wanting to get paid."

I wonder if that's how she greeted people spreading the Gospel of Jesus at her door. She reminded me of George Bailey's mother during the dream sequence in *It's A Wonderful Life* when he went to his old house and George's mother answered the door, but now it was a boarding house because George had never been born.

I guess I could have just said, "No problem, this one's on the house," but if I'd survived those two cranky old codgers, I could get through her. I was surprised when she came back with the money and more surprised that she didn't throw it at me. I wished I had one of the baskets on a pole from church, so I could collect her money and avoid eye contact. We had ticket receipts the size of postage stamps that came in sheets, and we tore one ticket off each week and handed it to the customer. My newspaper tickets, Mom's S&H stamps, Dad's postage stamps, I was joining in some family fun. I was able to control my tremors enough to tear it off and drop it in her rigid, impatient palm.

The next week, I wanted to show her she couldn't intimidate me, so I brought Steve along. *You want a piece of me, Mrs. Mazilli? Talk to my brother.* When she answered the door this time, she was pleasant and paid as if it were a voluntary donation. Steve took a good look at her, and if she was ever going to pick shells at Lake Antoine, look out.

A customer on one of Robert's paper routes was a heavy drinker and usually half in the bag when Robert showed up to tap into his booze fund. One day, the guy's wife let Robert in the kitchen, and the drunk, seated at the table, looked at Robert, and in that slurring, half-in-the-bag speech, said, "Why don't you shut up?" That didn't faze Robert. He showed up again the following week. By himself.

Real, Not Fake

After the ebony and ivory television was in the scrap heap, Mom and Dad would let us stay up on Saturday nights, so we could watch wrestling at 10:30 p.m. in living color. That was the best time on summer nights, too, for another family favorite, *The Tonight Show* with Johnny Carson. The Saturday night "rasslin" show was *All Star Wrestling* showcasing promoter (and wrestler) Verne Gagne's American Wrestling Alliance, or AWA, out of Minneapolis. Some of its stars were Nick Bockwinkel, Baron Von Raschke, the Crusher, and Mad Dog Vachon. In those days, the big arena matches were never on television. Promoters wanted paying rear ends in those arena seats, so they teased us with television studio wrestling shows. The *All Star Wrestling* ring was in a cramped studio. There were about ten times as many seats in the studio as there had been for the graduates at Mom's high school commencement, so there were about twenty folding chairs for twenty lucky fans.

The movie *The Wrestler* was released in 1974. Obviously, it wasn't actor Mickey Rourke's 2008 bittersweet tale of redemption of the same title. This was the original, a typical 1970s cheese-fest of a movie. Cheesy enough for my cooking-challenged brother Steve to put it on a burger and flip it in a frying pan. And, of course, we had ringside movie seats, basking in curds and whey. That flick had all the AWA stars, and I'm sure the holes in the movie plot were big enough to drive a truck through. And if you did, I bet one of the wrestlers would have distracted the referee.

Gamma ray radiation from a new source, cable television and station WKBD out of Detroit, stunted our growth in the mid '70s. On Saturday morning, WKBD televised *Roller Derby* followed by *Big Time Wrestling*. All I remember about *Roller Derby* was two teams on roller skates zipping around an elevated oval track with padded guardrails. I don't remember the rules, but do I remember that slamming someone into the rails or throwing them over brought cheering and scoring. Unfortunately for Raquel Welch, *The Godfather* was released in 1972, so her roller derby movie *Kansas City Bomber* from the same year got lost in the Oscar shuffle. We didn't go to Raquel's movie, we were too young to taste that provolone. It seemed like every week *Roller Derby* showed the Los Angeles Thunderbirds against some hapless team. The only skater I remember was Earlene Brown, a big, black woman who weighed well over two hundred-fifty pounds and wore number 747. Other skaters would bounce off her and go "*Boeing.*"

Earlene had won the bronze medal in the shot put for the United States at the 1960 Rome Olympics. I wonder if, while at the Rome games, she visited the soccer venue, *Stadio Flaminio*. Although that was our favorite stadium in the world, we couldn't confirm if there were any good magazine hiding spots inside. Surely, some *bambinos* figured out ways inside without paying with their own *lire*. In 2005, Earlene was posthumously inducted into the National Track and Field Hall of Fame during the Jesse Owens Awards and Hall of Fame Induction Ceremony. At least Earlene, unlike Jesse, hadn't been reduced to racing against horses after her Olympic career was over.

Big Time Wrestling was affiliated with the National Wrestling Alliance, the NWA. Some of their top wrestlers were the Mighty Igor, the Sheik, Bobo Brazil and my favorite, Pampero Firpo, the wild man from the pampas of Argentina. Firpo was a short, stocky guy with a hairy body, wiry black hair, and a long, scraggly beard. His trademark saying was a drawn out "Ooohhh yeaahhhh" in his gravelly voice. I thought Robert would look like Firpo when he got older. I wasn't too far off. The summer after college, Robert had a job with the Post Office delivering mail for vacationing mailmen. I think he was trying to beat the old man at his own game — paging Dr. Freud. Unlike Dad, though, he didn't have to take a test for his letter carrying job. When the regular mailman on one route returned from vacation, an old man asked him who was the Mexican delivering while he was gone. The guys at the Post Office got a kick out of that, so they started calling Robert "Chico."

As it turned out, Robert and Firpo were kindred spirits. In 1986, the year Robert worked as a summer letter carrier, Pampero Firpo retired from wrestling and began working for the U.S. Postal Service.

Grandpa Flaminio showed up a lot of Saturdays around the time *Big Time Wrestling* was on. It was such a coincidence. When wrestling came on, Grandpa showed up, like a cat hearing the electric can opener. He never visited during *Roller Derby*. Maybe that was special T.V. time for him and Grandma, but she drew the line at "fake wrestling." Grandpa didn't watch wrestling in the standard Flaminio TV viewing position. He sat in a chair, and his mouth was closed.

Just a few years ago, I was working in Cleveland when a contractor saw my last name was Flaminio; he asked me if I was from Iron Mountain, Michigan. I was surprised someone in Ohio knew the family. He told me he had spent a couple years in Iron Mountain as a kid, and his friend was Dan Flaminio, Dad's cousin. He told me that Dan's family was the first in the neighborhood to get television in the 1950s, and he remembered every Saturday morning going over there because they always watched professional wrestling. Professional wrestling must be in our DNA. You know, that sounds like a wrestler's finishing move (Oh no, Igor has put the Sheik in "The DNA." He's twisting him like a double-helix strand of nucleic acids!). Then again, genetics is probably thinking way outside the box for the Mighty Igor.

Igor's schtick was an "intellectually challenged" Polish wrestler. He wore long underwear beneath his wrestling trunks. He always had a big, goofy grin, like mine at the soda bottling plant and would wave to the fans with that fluttering little kid's wave. He'd even bring a kielbasa to some of his matches and share it with fans. I remember seeing him interviewed on TV, gnawing on a big Polish sausage.

Imagine our luck and excitement when *Big Time Wrestling* scheduled a card at the National Guard Armory in Kingsford! Steve, Carter, Robert, and I went and actually paid to get in. The headline match was Mighty Igor against Ben Justice.

The Armory gym was jam-packed and before the match, and Igor went through the crowd shaking hands. The fans went wild. If he had been running for President, he'd have had Dickinson County's vote locked up. We were all Polish that night.

During the match, Justice stabbed the Mighty Igor with a slim silver rod that looked like a pen. He'd stab Igor then quickly hide it in his wrestling trunks. Like everyone in the crowd, we went nuts. We tried to help the ref, pointing and screaming, "It's in his shorts! It's in his shorts!" The ref would look confused and finally search where everyone was pointing, but not before Justice would take the pen out and hide it in his boot. Then we'd scream, "It's in the boot! It's in the boot!" and the referee Mr. Clueless would finally look in the boot, but not before Houdini removed it and put it back in his shorts. That ref was so blind; he missed so many blatant rulebook violations, I bet he never worked another match again. In the end, the Mighty Igor was too strong and justice prevailed. Justice did not.

After the matches were over, the wrestlers sat at a long table signing autographs. Ben Justice's pen he was signing programs with looked awfully suspicious. I wished the referee were there, so I could say, "Do you see it NOW?"

Brothels and Spirits

We weren't the first Flaminios wreaking havoc on Hughitt Street. In the early 1900s, our predecessors left their marks up on the 100 block of West Hughitt Street. Angelo Flaminio (known as Butch) and Teresa Caretto (Jenny) married in 1898. He immigrated from Amorosi, Italy, a small town near Naples, and his first job in Iron Mountain was swinging a pick axe in an underground iron ore mine. After a cave-in left him and other miners trapped for three days, he quit his job and operated a saloon near the corner of West Hughitt and Carpenter Avenue. It's still there. Butch and Jenny had eight children — Pete, Dominic (they called him Patty), Ernest (Stubby), Art (my grandfather), Albert (Jumbo), Oscar, Madeleine (Madge), and Rosina. They lived in an apartment above the bar. Angie Godin's family store, Revolta's, was next door to Butch's saloon.

The stretch from the 100 to 300 block of West Hughitt Street was called the Midway. I guess you could call the Midway "The Las Vegas" of early Iron Mountain; it had several saloons and brothels, so if you wanted to find a politician in turn of the century Iron Mountain, you knew where to look. When the lumberjacks, mostly Swedes and French Canadians, came to town after toiling in the pines, they made a beeline for the Midway— and not for the free lunch buffets. After a few days on the Midway, a lot of them were broke and couldn't pay the train fare back to the sticks. Someone would always loan them money knowing they'd return with their paychecks to blow on booze and broads and debts. A woman called French Rosie ran a Midway saloon with a brothel upstairs (keep it down up there, I'm trying to get drunk!) She was a dice hustler and a standard deduction on a lumberjack paycheck. Her husband Norm played the piano in her saloon and was a regular, cheerful patron at Butch's place (Norm!). I guess when Norm told his wife he was going out for a drink she really couldn't argue with him. Norm always showed up at Butch's with a hand-rolled cigarette balancing on his lower lip. He didn't have to send his kids to Revolta's store to pick up a pack of smokes for him. After quenching his thirst with a few beers, he'd go back to Rosie's and pound at the piano. The pounding upstairs was the Swedes jacking lumber.

"Big Liz" ran another brothel on the Midway. She was well known throughout Upper Michigan and as far as Green Bay, Wisconsin. (This was before the Green Bay Packers, so if a black guy was in Iron Mountain no one asked him if he played professional football. He was probably just a worker.)

When he was a lad, Jumbo Flaminio worked at a Midway bakery. He'd remove his shoes and socks and highstep barefooted up and down the dough to knead it. I'm sure it wasn't the Holsum Bread we ate in the '70s and I'm certain baked bread wasn't stored in plastic bags back them, so those turn of the century Flaminio kids must have worn paper boots.

Working in a bakery was more wholesome than Stubby Flaminio's childhood vocation; he was the errand boy for Big Liz and her "ladies." When Liz paid him, he had to bring back his little bank book to prove he had deposited his earnings. Over the years, Stubby built up a nice-sized savings account. He learned frugality and the value of money from Big Liz and later bought stock in dime store S.S. Kresge (rebranded as K-Mart in the '70s), held it for decades, and profited handsomely. I don't know if the worldly experience on which she mentored Stubby was limited to finance, but I do know that Big Liz did not give him his nickname. The madam of another house of ill-repute on the Midway kept a parrot in a cage on the front porch. Whenever a potential John walked up to the madam's house, the parrot would cackle, "Ma! Ma! Another customer." When the kids in the neighborhood teased the bird, the lady of the house bolted out with a broom and shooed the kids away. Pet birds must have been popular back then. Grandpa told us when he was a kid, he had a pet crow he called Jimmy. He said it could talk, too. It must not have been against the law for Grandpa to have his crow Jim.

Sure, maybe there was a dearth of chastity on the Midway, but if someone was down on their luck or a civic cause needed money, the ladies were more than generous with their charity.

~~~

One day, Pete Flaminio heard shouting in a nearby saloon, so he ran over and lay on his stomach beneath the swinging doors to have a look. A lumberjack was standing against a wall daring anyone to take him on. Carter, was that you in a previous incarnation? A few tough guys signed his dance card. Though the lumberjack put up a good fight, they felled him like a jack pine and stomped him on the floor. Pete ran back and told his Dad what had happened and was told to mind his own business. That's what they meant by "don't ask, don't tell" in those days. There was a rumor in town that the lumberjack was killed and buried in the woods like a largemouth bass.

One of the Midway characters was a man with two cork legs they called Tom Corks. It's too bad he wasn't around for that party Mom and Dad threw; one of his legs would have come in handy for the broken couch. Tom Corks tacked flattened Prince Albert tobacco tins to his legs, painless body piercing. He made money doing odd jobs like polishing brass in saloons and selling little American flags at parades.

One day during World War I, Butch went out to sell War Bonds and left his sons Dominic and Art in charge of the saloon. When he returned a few hours later, the only person in the bar was dancing-challenged Tom, who was corked. Butch went upstairs and found Art passed out and Dominic in bed. Butch never disciplined the boys when they were in bed, so Dominic was pretending to sleep (likely in a spinning bed). Art wasn't playing make-believe. This is what happened when you sang drinking songs with Tom Corks: "Yo ho ho and a bottle of rum."

On the dark day in America when wine, women and song lost one-third of its appeal, and Prohibition became law, the coppers showed up at Butch's saloon, dragged the barrels of Italian vintage into the alley, and knocked them over. The neighbors swooped in with pitchers and harvested the ambrosia seeping from the barrels. Butch should have asked Tom Corks to bung the leaks with his legs. He sold near beer for about a year after going dry, but like most saloons, went out of business. From then on, if you wanted to enjoy some booze, you had to go to Al Capone's gangsters "Wartyback and Monkeyface, see."

Butch stacked wood behind the building for the saloon and apartment stoves. One Saturday, with the town abuzz for the circus in town, the boys were chopping wood. Butch peeked through the saloon window now and then to check up on them. One time when he looked, he saw only Stubby sitting on a sawhorse. Butch went out and asked where the other boys were. Stubby said he didn't know, so Butch told him to scoot. A little while later, the circus parade came down Carpenter Avenue. A lumberjack (probably broke, but happy) burst into the saloon and told Butch to come out and see his boys. Jumbo was on an elephant, and Art followed him in a chariot, dressed like a Roman general and driving a team of white horses. When they went by the saloon, Angelo gave them the "Italian Salute" for skipping out on their chores. The boys knew when they got home they'd have to scurry upstairs and get some pretend sleep.

Grandpa Flaminio once asked Steve, Carter, and me if we

wanted to bring up the tail end of a parade to shovel the horse manure. I have no idea who asked Grandpa if he knew anyone to be poop wranglers. Maybe after he rode that chariot down Carpenter Avenue, he became the go-to-guy for parade matters. No thanks, Ben Hur. Some of Steve's friends took that crappy job, and it turned out they were one of the most popular entrants in the parade.

LeFebvre's saloon was on the corner of Hughitt and Carpenter. In Iron Mountain it was Americanized to sound like "LaFave." Maybe the LeFebvre forbearers left Nova Scotia on the Cajun express with Brett Favre's phonetically challenged ancestors. Leo LeFebvre, the bar keep's boy, liked wearing clown costumes made by his mom. Did she make him a red-circled clown smock like my mom made me in Head Start? Leo really took his clowning to heart and entertained parade goers for decades in Iron Mountain. I remember Leo The Clown, walking up and down the route and making people laugh. Unlike Bozo The Clown, I don't ever remember him dropping F-bombs. The year our Impala station wagon wound up in the parade, was Leo was right in front of us, walking and waving, and, worriedly glancing over his shoulder wondering what was with that car with all the kids?

The Dickinson County Historical Society has a museum with displays from early Iron Mountain, including Leo's clown costume. They never asked for my Head Start clown costume. The museum is located in an old Carnegie Library, one of the many impressive stone and masonry buildings built all over America by industrialist Andrew Carnegie. He made his fortune in the steel industry in the early 1900s, when molten iron oozed from huge coal-fired blast furnaces. Someone had to shovel coal into those furnaces, and it wasn't Carnegie's mom.

In the summer of 1979, Iron Mountain celebrated its centennial. The historical society buried a time capsule next to the library for the bi-centennial in 2079. I know exactly where it is because I dug the hole for it.

The time capsule was a copper can. The capsule vault was just a steel garbage can set in concrete poured in the hole I dug. After a brief ceremony in which the museum curator presented the items of interest from 1979, he placed them in the can and saw there was still a lot of space. He asked people in the crowd if they had anything they'd like to contribute, and some old ladies offered up their Bibles and New Testaments. They didn't complain about fried-fish or cigar odors. Nothing says "1979 in Iron Mountain" like 3,000-year-old stories from Palestine. A July 1979 *Playboy* would have been appropriate and inappropriate at the same time. I wished I had a photo of me digging the hole so in a hundred years when they open the capsule, they could wonder "Who is this skinny kid with the shovel?" The copper can was sealed and set in the garbage can—er, vault —and called good for one hundred years.

Tough Cannoli

Like a lot of mining towns in Upper Michigan in the late 1800s and early 1900s, Iron Mountain overflowed with Italian immigrants. Our family, the Crispignas, Spigarellis, Pozzas, Santinis, and Carollos (and many more than I can mention) are the legacies to the Italians who came to barter sweat and labor for a better life. There was an old Italian immigrant saying, "I came to America because I heard the streets were paved with gold. When I got here I found out three things: first, they were not paved with gold; second, they were not paved at all; and third, I was expected to pave them." In Iron Mountain, they toiled in the iron mines and worked as stone masons, tile setters, shoe cobblers, and store keepers.

When your livelihood is back breaking labor, there is a natural desire to blow off some steam after stoking the engines, as evident by the following passage from a *Marquette Mining Journal* article titled "Doughty Dagoes" from 1888:

"At Nestoria yesterday 40 or 50 Italians who had been working on the extension boarded the train for Marquette. They were a noisy lot and filled the smoking car full. Some of them made a break for the first class coaches but brakeman Jones interfered, as there were ladies in those cars. The result was a lively battle. Jones got his head knocked through the window of the car door and retaliated by arming himself with a stove shaker and cracking a few Italian top knots, in a highly satisfactory manner."

Thank God, Casey Jones was there to protect those dainty, virtuous women from the garlic-breathing barbarian horde.

When Marie was in junior high school, she took a dishwashing job at Romagnolis, an Italian restaurant on Iron Mountain's north side, or the "nort" side, as the locals called it. The north side Italians were a fiercely loyal group. According to the north side story, they were the real Italians in Iron Mountain; just ask them. Italians from the center of town or the west side (like us) were called "Downtown Italians" in the early 1900s. My grandfather said back in the day, when the "Downtown Italians" would go to the north side, there would usually be some scuffles. It's funny that a small town like Iron Mountain had rival "ethnic" factions. New York City had the Sharks and Jets; Iron Mountain had the Goombas and Dagos.

Dwight Romagnoli, a big Italian guy who played football at Michigan State, owned the restaurant. Before it was Romagnolis, the place was known as Irish's. I think only Catholics could own it. Dwight later built a larger restaurant on the highway at the edge of town. Every summer, my brother Steve brings some of his co-workers up to his summer home in Spread Eagle, Wisconsin, about ten miles from Iron Mountain, for a four-day golf vacation. His lakeside getaway is near the strip joint in Spread Eagle. It's tradition the first night's dinner is at Romagnolis.

During one dinner, Dwight told us a story about his 1965 Kingsford High basketball team that made it to the Michigan high school semi-finals. They played River Rouge, a Detroit high school. Teams from Upper Michigan making it so far in the state basketball tournament, let alone winning, were few and far between. Detroit, Flint, and Saginaw players were more talented than short, white kids from Upper Michigan, so their schools dominated the tournament. Dwight told us his team was just a bunch of kids happy to stay in a hotel and eat at a restaurant. They played the Kingsford-River Rouge game at the Lansing Everett High School gym, where Magic Johnson would become a high school star a decade later. The game involved two towns with rich Ford Motor Company traditions. In the 1920s, Henry Ford built a sawmill and a parts factory in Kingsford to manufacture wooden components for his automobiles, the "woodies." During World War II, it manufactured the Waco wooden gliders that transported troops on D-Day.

I didn't know it at the time, but Bob "Shutters" Hartline, who was the official photographer at Iron Mountain Mountaineer sporting events, had served in the 325th Glider Infantry Regiment attached to the 82nd Airborne Division during World War II. Shutters landed in Normandy on D-Day on a Waco glider, and after thirty-one days of combat without replacements, his company was down to one officer and five enlisted men. All the time I knew Shutters and saw him on the sideline at football games snapping pictures, I never imagined that he was a glider infantryman in World War II. That seemed to be common for World War II vets; they came home, got on with their lives and didn't talk much about their experiences.

The Ford factory shut down in 1951. At one time, wooden autos were a revolutionary idea, but it was a doomed concept after advances in metallurgy, plastics, and fiberglass. Maybe Dutch footwear and spoon manufacturers think wood is good, but it's not for modern transportation.

When the factory was running, Ford used the scrap wood to make charcoal. When it closed, the sawmill and charcoal operation were sold to local businessmen. Anyone who barbeques in America the correct way, the way San Lorenzo would approve, knows the name Kingsford Charcoal. A large corporation later bought the charcoal operations and the plant closed in 1961, but Kingsford briquettes live on.

The Ford River Rouge complex was at one time the largest integrated factory in the world. It was 1.5 miles long by 1-mile wide, and in the 1930s it employed over 100,000 workers. Over four decades, it produced the American icon, the Ford Mustang. The 1965 Kingsford High basketball team was just a bunch of football players who happened to play basketball. They muscled their way to a half-time lead against the Motor City boys. Detroit fans didn't take too kindly to these "Canadians" from above the Mackinac Bridge whooping them in the first half, and they were getting a little unruly. Dwight said that before half time, one of the referees pointed to an exit and told them that if they won they needed to run through that door as fast as they could.

After the final buzzer, the Kingsford boys casually walked through the door. River Rouge's talent was too much.

Cosell, Gifford, and Ho Chi Minh

In the early 1970s, the Vietnam War hung thick in the nation's consciousness. I was fairly attuned to the war, more so than most boys my age. We subscribed to *Newsweek*, and I would thumb through it for articles on the war. Like a lot of people, we watched the *CBS Evening News* with Walter Cronkite ("and that's the way it was") every day after dinner. There were usually reports from Dan Rather or Morley Safer in Vietnam. Whenever Mom saw Dan Rather on T.V., she'd shriek "Ooh, I'd rather Dan." I worried that I would be drafted when I finished high school, but Mom and Dad assured me that the war would be over by the time I graduated. They were prophetic when it came to wars and comets.

Dad's brother Jerry served with the U. S. Air Force in Da Nang, but the war didn't touch any families that I can remember in our neighborhood. Most of the older kids in our neighborhood graduated high school in 1971 or later, and by then, the draft had ended. By 1973, American troops had pulled out of Vietnam and a Laotian sprinter had his passport stamped for the States and the hundred yard dash.

One morning I was walking to school and a kid from my school was on the sidewalk on the opposite side of the street. He was carrying something in his hand, and I asked him what it was. "It's a letter to my Dad in Saigon," he said. So his Dad was in the military or in some foreign service position. He was the only other person I knew with a family member there.

Several people from the area served in Vietnam. Martin Neuens, a U.S. Air Force Academy graduate and an F-105 fighter-bomber pilot, graduated from Kingsford High School in 1959, one year after Dad. He was shot down in 1966 and held in a North Vietnamese prison, finally being released in 1973 with all the POWs. When he returned to Kingsford, the town held a big parade for him; it seemed everyone in the area turned out for it. Our family sat along Woodward Avenue, right in front of the Woodward Bar.

We watched on television when the POWs returned from North Vietnam. It was called Operation Homecoming, and Clark Field in the Philippines was the first stop for the flights dubbed the "Hanoi Taxis." Like most of the country, we sat glued to our TV sets as the planes landed at Hickam Field in Hawaii, and the former prisoners walked down the ramp from the plane as their families rushed the tarmac to greet them. It was a very emotional experience, watching those pilots hug their wives and sons and daughters for the first time after years of captivity. Now, that was must see TV.

A humorous side note on the Vietnam War (if there is such a thing). We watched ABC Monday Night Football in the 1970s, a weekly ritual for a lot of families back then. The Pittsburgh Steelers were playing, and one of their running backs, Rocky Bleier, had played college ball at Notre Dame and served in Vietnam where he was wounded. After healing, he made a heroic comeback to professional football. During the game, the venerable announcer Howard Cosell rattled on and on about Bleier's story, going to Vietnam, the injury, and the comeback. He ended his soliloquy with "...and the doctors said he would never play football again." Don Meredith, the color commentator, without missing a beat and in his Texas twang shot back, "The North Vietnamese said that too!" I still laugh at that one.

Don Meredith played quarterback for the Dallas Cowboys in the 1960s. His center for a lot of those years was Dave Manders, Dad's schoolmate. Dave played college ball at Michigan State; his first season with Dallas was in 1964, and he played eleven seasons for coach Tom Landry. However, he didn't play in the famous "Ice Bowl" on December 31, 1967 against the Packers, not even half-a-Bowl, because he was injured and had missed the entire season. He was starting center for the Cowboys team that beat the Miami Dolphins in the '72 Super Bowl. Once Dad took Steve and me to Manders' parents' house in Kingsford to meet him. I shook his hand, and his meaty paw engulfed my bony fingers. He took off his Super Bowl ring and let me try it on. It was big, heavy, gold and studded with diamonds, no chance of a Flaminio breaking it or losing it in some hot lunch beta carotene. I put it on my thumb, and it just hung there.

Since Dad's friend played for the Cowboys, they were my second favorite team after the Packers. One Christmas, Dad gave Steve and me helmets— no, not the brother Tony helmet-like haircuts; Steve got a Packer helmet, and I got a Cowboy helmet. I brought mine to show-and- tell at school in a brown paper bag. Unlike Carter and his "telescope," Mom didn't interrogate me when I left the house with my show-and-tell prop.

In my classes' show-and-tell, you would go to the front of the class with your hidden item and give clues to your classmates, so they could guess what it was. We didn't stick our hand in a hole for a guess like for Carter's show-and-tell. I let one of my classmates peak in my bag before my turn, and he took a good look at the silver helmet with the big, blue Texas star emblem. When I was in front of the class, no one could guess what it was, so I called on my "audience plant." "It's a Bart Starr helmet," he said with the assuredness of answering a teenage birthday card riddle. Ugh! If I had a Cleveland Brown helmet, and he was marginally aware of Jim Brown, we could have pulled it off.

Equal Rights, Squatter's Rights

In the '70s, kids played baseball games on empty lots all over town. We played on the corner lot outside the stadium's east wall, the skating rink. It had a ready-made home run wall; the only bad thing was if someone jacked one, you had to go in the stadium to retrieve it, facing possible centerfold distraction.

In the mid 1970s, the Cincinnati Reds were the best team in baseball. I was a fair-weather baseball fan and didn't follow the major leagues as closely as Patti McGuire turn-ons, so I had no problem jumping on the Red's bandwagon. Pete Rose, Johnny Bench, Tony Perez, Joe Morgan, and Dave Concepcion were my favorite players. Coming from a family of ten kids, it made sense liking a baller named Concepcion. I was the second pregnancy in the family, so I was the baseball player known as Segundo Concepcion.

We played in organized baseball leagues, starting with Pee Wee baseball, our T-ball league. I played third base for a few games and had a rough time throwing to first base. There was no telling where the ball would end up. The coaches tried to tinker with my throwing motion if there would ever be a chance of me getting it to first. They just threw up their hands and told me to roll the ball to first base. Roll it? Why don't you just get a girl to take my position? But I was a team player, so I rolled the ball to first base. I became the best bocce ball player in Pee Wee. Maybe they should have put me at pitcher. Since there was a tee, a player just stood on the pitcher's mound and waited for balls to dribble to him. After he caught it, it was a short roll to first.

Once you turned nine years old, you were pushed out of the Pee Wee nest. That's when we would try out for a Little League team. Most of our teams were sponsored by places where men gathered — Elks, Rotary, Kiwanis, UCT (United Commercial Travelers). Why didn't the local strip joint have a team? The Immaculate Conception Church had a team too. Like the church, the team was just called "I.C." No, their baseball uniforms weren't altar boy smocks. I would have played for them if they'd changed their name to the Dave Concepcion Church.

If you didn't make a Little League team, you could play Minor League baseball, a league sponsored by the community recreation program. It was real baseball, a pitcher throwing to a batter, or in my case rolling to a batter. But since this wasn't a cricket league, I couldn't be a pitcher. Maybe I should have checked with all those Indian and Pakistani doctors in town to see if they had a cricket league. We didn't have uniforms in this league; we just wore blue jeans and a t-shirt that said "Community Schools Minor League Baseball." Face it; we got to wear t-shirts that proudly proclaimed we weren't good enough for Little League. So what, it was still a fun league; there were even some girls playing. At that time, there weren't any girls good enough to play Little League, like all the boys in Minor League baseball.

Marie played one summer of Minor League. She was in right field during one game, lost in her own little world performing an "arm ballet," oblivious to the game. It looked like she was waving in a 747 jetliner. The other team didn't mind because the Black Swan never saw the ball that landed in front of her and rolled by. It finally dawned on her that the screaming she heard wasn't her imaginary audience cheering her crowning as Miss America (Why is pageant emcee Bert Parks saying, "Get the ball, Get the ball?"). When I was eleven, my throwing improved where I could throw a baseball in a Comet Kahoutek-like trajectory, and I made the Elks. When I was twelve, no one wanted to play catcher, so I volunteered. Even though I had only one good eye, I thought I'd be a decent catcher. In 1975, the unthinkable happened — a girl, Michelle Gendron, made the Elks. She deserved to be a teammate; she was as good as any boy on the team, especially one-eyed wonders. Appropriately, the team whose namesake was an animal with a rack had the first girl player. The odds were good that Team Vatican in our league wouldn't have the first girl. I welcomed her on our team. I was catcher; she was in the outfield. As long as she could field and hit more power to her.

Our coaches discovered after a few games that a Cyclops catcher is one dimensional. After a pitch, I would close my eyes (or make that eye), and wish the pitch into my mitt. When the batter swung and missed, there was no telling where the ball would end up. It didn't take too long for the coaches to give me the hook and move Michelle from left field to catcher. Now there would be someone new squatting behind home plate. My throws to second base to nail a base stealer were better than hers, but she could catch a pitch a lot better than me. That's a good skill to have for a catcher. I took her place in left field. Were the coaches really concerned about the play in left field, and that's why they had us switch positions? Yeah, that's it.

Little League had certain rules that never accounted for girl players. The league was about balls (and strikes). Just a few years ago, if you had said there would be girls playing, they'd call you nuts. Protective cups are required by league regulations. Our coach sheepishly handed Michelle her cup the first practice after she was demoted to catcher. At least I got to keep my cup and was free to do with it what I always did at home, put it up to my face and say, "Look, an oxygen mask."

~~~

When Carter and I played for the Elks, Mom and Dad bought us new baseball gloves. Mine had red, white, and blue webbing. It's the kind of glove that guarantees a spot on the office softball team if you're an intern at Fox News. Carter got an aqua-blue glove, likely not a Vida Blue autograph model. He would have looked good in the outfield with my knit pilot hat. Carter had the only blue glove in Little League. I don't think anyone had blue balls.

These weren't second hand gloves either; they were Rawlings, the best. If Mom had rummaged for our gloves, with her luck she would have found me a four fingered glove from the 1890s (but it's signed by Lord Byron!). Our gloves were more of the nice things Mom and Dad bought for us, even though we were on a tight budget.

Carter's glove was stolen after a pickup baseball game at the Westside ball field. Naturally, Mom wasn't happy. More than anything, it was about the money spent on that glove. We weren't going to lose the blue rawhide without putting up a fight. Mom loaded Carter, Robert, a few others, and me into the Impala station wagon for a glove hunt. If we found the kid who took it, Carter would be looking to improve his slugging percentage.

If the thief was playing somewhere, we would have found him because that blue glove was hard to miss. We were blind, not colorblind. After our reconnaissance at the Westside field turned up nothing, we scoured every other ball field in Iron Mountain. Empty handed, we headed to Kingsford. Mom was shaking down some kids at the ball field behind the Woodward Bar. One kid told Mom no one there took the glove. She balked. Without her wooden spoon, she couldn't bring the hammer down. However, it would have been funny seeing her chase one of them down the first base line with that spoon. That would have been historically accurate because Mom had a wooden spoon, not an aluminum one.

As the vanquished in the "loser leave town match," we went

home gloveless. Now Carter and I would have to share my glove. I wasn't sure how we could play left field with both our hands up my mitt. Poor Carter, even bare-foot Joe Jackson had a glove. We never did find that blue beauty. Maybe the person who took it was getting married and needed the glove to complete the "something old, something new" wedding poem. That glove wasn't the "something borrowed" gift because Carter never got it back.

The Labor Pool

If any of our neighbors had a dirty job, they knew where they could hire some Italian peasants. They all paid a fair wage too, for the most part. When I was around fourteen, the Markells, who lived a block down the alley from us, were putting in a swimming pool. Not a full below-ground pool, just partially below ground, like Grandma Hazus' pool (minus the plankton). Mrs. Markell said she'd pay Carter, Robert, and me three bucks an hour, a decent wage, to dig the hole for the pool.

Mrs. Markell had a beautiful reddish-orange 1966 Mustang convertible. She was a good golfer with a slender figure and wore shorts and sleeveless blouses in the summer. As I said, I was fourteen at the time, the age boys tune into those things. The operative word would be "cherry." I'm talking about the car.

The summer sun was beating hard that day. We were working like dogs and drenched in sweat; I had to take my shirt off. Maybe Mrs. Markell would like that. Probably not — I was a skinny kid. We were three abreast, shoveling hunched over with our sweaty, blistered hands slipping along the wooden shafts. It was just like the prison chain gang movie, *Cool Hand Luke*, "I got a shovel over here boss!" Maybe Mrs. Markell would wash her Mustang with a bucket of warm, soapy water. Maybe she would sponge the ragtop and while reaching across press her suds-soaked upper body against the driver's side window. When we finished, Mom stopped by to make sure we had satisfied Mrs. Markell. She told Mom about the three dollar hourly wage, and Mom retorted "Oh, no." We were worn out, sweaty, and dirty, but our spirits lifted, seeing Mom play hardball with Mrs. Markell; maybe she'd demand a better wage. "You only have to pay them two dollars an hour," Mom told her. Huh?! The Markells were putting in a pool; I'm sure they could afford three dollars an hour. Unfortunately, Mrs. Markell accepted the counter offer. Mom must have wanted to teach us lesson. Apparently the lesson was that two dollars is thirty-three percent less than three dollars. Jimmy Hoffa wept.

Our collective bargaining outcome was disappointing, considering Dad was a member of the AFL-CIO affiliated National Association of Letter Carriers. He had also walked the picket line during the Recreation Lanes pinsetter wildcat strike of 1954. In those days, teenage boys reset the pins. They'd sit on an elevated bench behind the pins, and when they were knocked down, they'd spring into action. They'd jump off the bench, lower a rack that grabbed the pins left standing, raise it, and then sweep away the pins knocked down. Then they'd re-lower the rack to reset the pins and hop back on the bench.

The owner, Pete Tomassoni, paid ten cents a game. Dad said that by the time they deducted charges for all the soda they drank and chips they ate, a lot of the boys had nothing left; some even owed Pete money.

Bowling was popular in the 1950s, and league nights were big moneymakers for the alley owners. One league night, one of the pinsetters declared they should make eleven cents a game, a ten percent raise at the drop of a dime. You see, Mom, the goal is to make the owner class pay you more money, not less. All the other boys were on board, and they told Pete the new labor terms. Either pay up, or they'd walk. He just laughed at them and told them to get back to work. The next strike that night wasn't on Lane 7. The pinsetters stood strong and walked out in the middle of league night. They just hung out on the sidewalk talking about ball sizes, and not the ones inside. The bowling came to a standstill, and Pete had a real conundrum on his hands. On one side, he had a bunch of junior high school kids shaking him down. On the other side, he had a bunch of angry, Blatz Beer-fueled bowlers ready to mutiny. Something had to give. The outcome still brings a joyous tear to a Longshoreman's eye.

They're still rolling strikes at Recreation Lanes, and it's still owned by the Tomassoni family. With automatic pinsetters today, they don't have to worry about work stoppages from teenage labor hooligans. Ironically, Mom later worked as a teacher's aide and represented the union in negotiations with the Board of Education. I hope her negotiating skills had improved since she represented the pool diggers local.

Finally...

Well, that's about it. The 1970s in all its glory in our little corner of Iron Mountain. The next thing you know, it's the 1980s and high school, college, Dexy's Midnight Runners, careers, marriages (and divorces), and kids. Mom and Dad raised ten kids on a mailman's salary and side jobs as a janitor and hot lunch cook, and they did it without ever owning one credit card. Lucky for us we had understanding neighbors, storeowners, doctors, dentists, and optometrists. And a teen-age girl with a free turkey.

Whenever I'm back in town, I always drive down Hughitt Street past the old home. It's not the same though. That saying, "You can never go home again," is true, but that's just the natural order of things. When I drive by, it's just a house. There isn't a pile of bikes lying on the ground, no owl tacked on the house, no kids perched on the roof (or jumping off it). Angie's high-pitched voice ("stay away from my grapes!") yells out no more. Her beautiful lilac bushes are gone. A fence surrounds the Ellingson's yard. At least the apple tree is outside it.

Busy with our own lives, jobs and families, the times are few and far between when all twelve of us gather. But when we do, one of these stories usually comes up, followed by good laughter and possibly a reenactment. As we get older, the memories fade a little, and we have to dig further down to find them. They're still there though, safely hidden in the deep recesses of consciousness; you just have to know where to look for them.

Like a rolled up *Playboy* inside a metal pipe.

Epilogue

Steve graduated from Central Michigan University with a degree in accounting. He is a finance director for Dow Chemical in Michigan and married to his high school sweetheart Mary Ann Crispigna. They have three daughters— Kaylie, Sydney and Alexie.

Marie graduated from Northern Michigan University with a degree in communications. She is a senior human resources manager at Eaton Corporation in Michigan. She has daughters Megan and Jenna.

Tom graduated from Michigan Technological University with a degree in chemical engineering. He is an engineer with AECOM in Michigan.

Vince (Carter) graduated from Michigan Technological University with a degree in accounting and has an MBA from DePaul University. He is a hospital administrator in Chicago. He is married to Anne Alder, and they have triplets — identical twin boys John and Vincent and daughter Isabella.

Kathy is a 911 operator in Minnesota (Giant Ice!). She is married to Todd Trahan and has daughters Malisa, Molly, and Macy and step-children Hannah and Sam.

Robert graduated from Northern Michigan University with

a degree in elementary education. He is a teacher in Michigan and married to Jill Aranowski. They have sons Paul and Ben and daughter Abby.

John graduated from Northern Michigan University with a degree in biology and chemistry. He is an operations manager for Veolia Environmental Services in Chicago and married to Angela Kinzer.

Jim graduated from Northern Michigan University with a degree in business administration. He is a sales representative for Glunz Beer in Chicago.

Tony graduated from Central Michigan University with a degree in accounting. He is the finance director for a mechanical contractor trade association in Minneapolis-St.Paul. He is married to Kathy Gradwohl, and they have a daughter Sophia and son Joshua.

Stephanie (Moomer) graduated from Northern Michigan University with a degree in Health Education and Saginaw Valley State University with a nursing degree. She is an OB/GYN nurse in Michigan and married to John Zacharski. They have daughters Zoey and Anna and sons Zack and Johnny.

Mom and Dad are enjoying retirement in the Iron Mountain area. Dad golfs four times a week and manages to squeeze in eight months of golf (some of it chilly) at local courses. Ever the crafter, Mom has carved out a niche making mittens from wool sweaters. A cigarette doesn't dangle from her mouth when she's stitching; she gave that up years ago.

Afterword

Once I surpassed the answer to my internet search "how many pages are in a book," I figured I was a stone's throw away from publishing. After hammering out numerous drafts, I went over every line in the book one last time— "Well, that's good. I don't see any problems," I thought.

Next I had to find a literary agent; that was another cyber-space discovery. I had to "query," or ask an agent to review my manuscript. After his or her review, the agent would sign me, hunt me a book deal, and take a 15% cut of the sales. Surely one query letter would do the trick, so I sent one to an agent who looked promising, based on the other humor authors he's represented. Like clockwork, he responded and asked for the complete manuscript. That's how it works, right? I was confident this was just a formality, and he'd say "Yep, looks fine. Sign here and we'll start printing."

Uh, not quite. The agent contacted me and said the manuscript wasn't for him, and suggested it be edited. I guess an unbiased fresh set of eyes are needed to root out the styling and grammar errors. I searched the internet for editors; there are a lot of them out there. I contacted Georganna Hancock from San Diego, and she told me to email her the manuscript so she could take a quick look at it to get an idea of the editing needed.

A few days later I called her. "I see you are from Iron Mountain," she said. "Did you know Leo LeFebvre." Surprised, I said "Well, yeah, he's in one of the chapters in the book." ("Are you kidding me," I thought to myself. "Is she playing a game?"). "I was married to his nephew. Leo's sister was my mother-in-law," Georganna said. I think that's when I heard *The Twilight Zone* theme music.

Georganna told me she had vacationed at the LeFebvre cabin on Moon Lake, outside Iron Mountain, and had seen the Pine Mountain ski jump; she also mentioned Leo being a parade clown. Of all the editors in America, I "randomly" selected the one related to a person in my book, and who had spent time in Iron Mountain. The eminent Swiss psychiatrist Carl Jung, the pioneer of the collective unconscious, coined the term "synchronicity," which is the experience of two events that are apparently unrelated, but are observed to occur together in a meaningful manner. Sting, meet *Synchronicity 3*.

Writer's often speak of their "Muse," a guiding spirit providing creative inspiration. The Muses were nine daughters of Zeus, each presiding over a different art. A Muse provides the sweet, syrupy prose when cerebral labor resembles the Myth of Sisyphus— endlessly pushing a boulder up a hill for no reason or reward. As Dante pleaded in *The Inferno*, "O Muses, O high genius, aid me now!"

I remember writing several passages where the words just flowed from my fingertips, producing a rhythmic rat-a-tat-tat on the keyboard. Was that me who was writing, or was someone writing through me?

Maybe it was my Muse, the same one who inspired some clown from Iron Mountain.

Works Cited

"Earlene Brown." *Wikipedia, The Free Encyclopedia.* Wikimedia Foundation, Inc., 04 Mar 2012. <http://en.wikipedia. org/Earlene Brown>

Immaculate Conception Church; St. Mary and St. Joseph Church, *Diocese of Marquette,* retrieved from *http://www. dioceseofmarquette.org/parishes* January 7, 2011.

"Jesse Owens." *Wikipedia, The Free Encyclopedia.* Wikimedia Foundation, Inc., 16 Feb 2012. <http://en.wikipedia. org/Jesse Owens>

"Juan Kachmanian (a.k.a. Pampero Firpo)." *Wikipedia, The Free Encyclopedia.* Wikimedia Foundation, Inc., 01Mar 2012. <http:/en.wikipedia.org/Juan Kachmanian>

"Mighty Igor." *Wikipedia, The Free Encyclopedia.* Wikimedia Foundation, Inc., 11 Feb 2011. <http://en.wikipedia.org/Mighty Igor>

"Tony Galento." *Wikipedia, The Free Encyclopedia.* Wikimedia Foundation, Inc., 28 Feb 2012. <http://en.wikipedia. org/Tony Galento>

Front: Jim, Kathy
Left to Right: John, Stephanie, Marie, Steve, Robert, Tony,
Mom, Dad, Tom, and Vince
Twins: Steve and Marie, Vince and Kathy, Jim and John,
Stephanie and Tony

Made in the USA
Monee, IL
03 August 2021

74904750R00125